Stop IT project failure
through risk management

Acknowledgement

This book is the result of many years' work with IT projects and discussions with IT practitioners, consultants, academics as well as with masters and doctoral students. The ideas presented in this book have been chewed over again and again in many different discussion forums. However there is one individual who has made a special contribution to the thinking in this book and that is Terry White. Therefore my special thanks goes to Terry White, whom I regard as one of the most progressive thinkers in information technology management today.

Dan Remenyi

Stop IT project failure through risk management

Dr Dan Remenyi

 Routledge
Taylor & Francis Group

LONDON AND NEW YORK

First published by Butterworth-Heinemann

First published 1999

This edition published 2011 by Routledge
2 Park Square, Milton Park, Abingdon, Oxon OX14 4RN
711 Third Avenue, New York, NY 10017, USA

Routledge is an imprint of the Taylor & Francis Group, an informa business

© Techtrans Limited 1999

TRADEMARKS/REGISTERED TRADEMARKS
Computer hardware and software brand names mentioned in this book are protected by their respective trademarks and are acknowledged.

British Library Cataloguing in Publication Data
A catalogue record for this book is available from the British Library

ISBN 0 7506 4503 2

Typeset by P.K.McBride, Southampton

Contents

About the author

Dr Dan Remenyi has spent more than 25 years working in the field of corporate computers and information systems. He has worked with computers as an IS professional, business consultant and as a user. In all these capacities he has been primarily concerned with benefit realisation and obtaining the maximum value for money from the organisations' information systems investment and effort. In recent years he has specialised in the area of the formulation and the implementation of strategic information systems and how to evaluate the performance of these and other systems. He has also worked extensively in the field of information systems project management, specialising in the area of project risk identification and management. He has written a number of books and papers in the field of IT management and regularly conducts courses and seminars as well as working as a consultant in this area. His most recent books include *Achieving Maximum Value from Information Systems – A Process Approach* and *Preparing and Evaluating a Business Case For IT Investment*.

He has work over the years for many organisations in different parts of the world both as a management consultant and as an executive development facilitator. These organisations include IBM, Barclays Bank, Ernst and Young, FI Group, Caterpillar Division of Barlows, Andersen Consulting, National Health Service in the UK, Spoornet (the national railroad company of South Africa), Liberty Life Insurance Company, and the Anglo Vaal Mining Corporation.

Dan Remenyi holds a B.Soc.Sc., an MBA and a PhD. He is a Visiting Professor at Chalmers University of Technology in Gothenberg, Sweden and an associate member of faculty at Henley Management College in the United Kingdom.

E-mail: remenyi@compuserve.com
World Wide Web: http://www.mot.chalmers.se/mcf/Staff/Da-re.html

How to use this book

This book offers practical hands-on type advice as to how to manage IS project risks.

The book consists of three sections.

The first section which comprises the first three chapters is a general background to IS Project Risks. It describes the nature of the risks which IS projects face and some ideas as to how these risks occur and what type of actions can be taken to ameliorate them.

The second section of the book, which begins with Chapter 4, is a framework for the identification and management of IS project risks which may be used as a practical hands-on approach to project risk management.

Chapter 11 is, unlike the other chapters, a case study which illustrates how the IS project risk framework described in the book may be used in practice.

The Appendices contain useful forms which may be used in implementing the framework described in the book.

Preface

This book is about information systems development failures and how to avoid them. It considers what goes wrong with information systems development projects and what actions may be taken to avoid potential difficulties. The reduction of the impact, or even the elimination of the problems, is discussed in terms of an information systems risk management programme.

To be successful at information systems application development it is essential to make risk management an integral part of the project management. If information systems risk management is treated as an add-on or an add-in it will simply slip between the cracks and not achieve its objectives.

The objective of information systems risk management is to ensure that information systems projects are completed successfully, and this is not a trivial task. A risk management process needs to be put in place and also needs continuous monitoring and continuous response. The primary purpose of these activities is to reduce the possibility of under-performance.

By its very nature the risk management process is complex. This is at least in part due to the fact that project management risks have at their centre, important behavioural implications. People and their behaviour are never simple and it is this dimension which makes risk management difficult.

However the day-to-day routine activities of the risk management process involve much of what is generally considered to be simply good management practices in the project arena. Thus ensuring that the objectives of the information systems project are fully and correctly understood, that appropriate information systems tools are chosen and that adequately trained staff are available, to mention only three of many issues, are routine but quite important elements of the risk management process. It is perhaps because there are many relatively routine issues involved in the risk management process that this most important aspect of information systems project management tends to be largely overlooked and sometimes completely ignored.

This book helps to ensure that IS project managers are successful in helping to deliver application systems. However, IS development risk can never be entirely eliminated and consequently the practitioner needs to bear in mind that an IS development project is never without risk, and hence there is a continuing potential for something to go wrong.

The book explains the key issues and variables and makes specific practical suggestions about the good management practice that is required to implement IS project risk processes.

Dan Remenyi

remenyi@compuserve.com

1 | Information systems project risk management

Risk management guides us over a vast range of decision-making, from allocating wealth to safeguarding public health, from waging war to planning a family, from paying insurance premiums to wearing a seatbelt, from planting corn to marketing cornflakes.

(Bernstein, 1996)

Building an information system, ... an online, distributed, integrated customer service system, ... is generally not an exercise in 'rationality'. It is a statement of war or at the very least a threat to all interests that are in any way involved with customer service.

(Laudon, 1989)

In preparing for battle I have always found that plans are useless, but that planning is indispensable.

(Dwight D. Eisenhower)

1.1   Introduction to information systems risks

Risk and the management thereof, in the context of information systems (IS) development, is an issue that has not received much attention. In general it has been assumed that the assumptions and estimates used in IS development plans would actually be realised and that there was no real need for much in the way of contingency provision or other courses of action to ensure success, or to prevent failure.

There have been many impressive information technology successes (Cash et al. 1992; Earl 1992). Some organisations have flourished because of the competitive advantages derived from the information systems that they have developed. Others have used information systems to improve the efficiency and the effectiveness of their organisation's operation. But at the same time there has also been a plethora of failures.

1.2 Information systems development failures

There have always been IS development failures, and some of these have been spectacular (Allingham et al., 1992). In the United Kingdom alone, the London Ambulance System, the Wessex Health Service, Taurus Financial Services are all well documented as suffering substantial failures costing huge amounts of money. However, there are many more instances that have not been brought to the public's attention and have consequently not been 'celebrated'. Of course it is not usual to celebrate failure, and in the process of sweeping the embarrassment of failure under the carpet, significant opportunity for learning is lost. It is difficult to obtain accurate statistics, but various sources suggest that a significant percentage of IS projects fail, of which the following are interesting examples.

During April 1994, insurance giant Prudential abandoned all further development of their five-year 'Plato' in-house project costing £40 million intended to downsize from mainframe to client-server architecture. A well-researched BBC documentary 'The Net' (broadcast on 18 May 1994) estimated that poorly managed and abandoned IT projects in British government departments alone had cost the taxpayer the equivalent of £5 billion over the previous twelve years. That is roughly £90 for every man, woman and child in the United Kingdom. The much vaunted 'Operational Strategy' project of the British Social Security department cost £2 billion and has delivered very little to date. One report states that: *"the project performed badly on all principal expectations held by its early decision-makers"* (Collins, 1994). Elsewhere in the United Kingdom, the Department of the Environment for Northern Ireland sued its supplier over a failed £8 million system. Ironically the dispute was settled by paying the supplier a further £1 million due to an extraordinary legal anomaly (Collins, 1994).

IS Project Risk

The bankruptcy trustee appointed to oversee the liquidation of FoxMeyer Corp. and FoxMeyer Drug Co. has sued the companies' software supplier, for $500 million for alleged gross negligence. In papers filed in the US District Court in Delaware, Bart Brown said the software vendors' alleged fraud and negligence, "led to the demise of FoxMeyer, a once-thriving $5 billion wholesale drug distribution company". According to the lawsuit, although the vendor had historically made software for manufacturing, the Walldorf, Germany-based company, "assured FoxMeyer that its R/3 system was well suited to the needs" of the high volume and complex price structure of FoxMeyer's distribution business. The system did not work and its failure, it is alleged, led to FoxMeyer going bankrupt. When the system was installed, its volume limitations made it useable at only six of FoxMeyer's 23 distribution warehouses, court papers said. "The failure of the system to perform as the vendor had represented…was a significant factor contributing to FoxMeyer's August 1996 bankruptcy and subsequent liquidation."

In the United States, the General Accounting Office found that the development of three '*severely flawed*' government systems continued for periods ranging from three to eight years at a cost of more than £19 million to US taxpayers before they were scrapped (Betts, 1992).

Although it is acknowledged that IS failure has become a common problem, there is no agreement on the actual percentage of projects that fail. This is complicated by difficulties with the definition of IS failure. Keil (1994) contends that the definition of computer failure depends on whom you ask. He reports that DeMarco (1982) says there is a 15% failure rate; Gladden (1982) found 75%, Lyytinen and Hirchheim (1987) say 50%; Crescenzi (1988) says 85% and Wilbern (1992) says 60%.

1.3   Definitions of information systems development failure

It is hard to establish a consensus of exactly what constitutes IS failure. There is little if any consistency in the literature as to the exact extent, or for that matter, the actual nature of IS failure. However, broadly stated, IS failures occur when IS projects do not achieve the expectations or objectives of the original user or system owners. But this explanation is too simple as the real problem lies in deciding when, and to what extent, those expectations or objectives have been met. However these issues are defined, failure is generally agreed to have occurred when a project has:

- commenced development, but was abandoned before completion;

- been fully developed, but never used;

- been fully developed and commissioned, but abandoned within a very short period of time;

- not been fully developed as originally envisaged, but substantially down-scaled until it no longer provides the originally envisaged functionality.

Of course there are lesser forms of failure i.e. degrees of failure, which occur when an unsuccessful IS project can still be rescued by additional, but unplanned application of resources. Then again the success of projects is sometimes measured by whether they are on-time, to budget and according to specification. Using these criteria Beam (1994) suggests that only 2% of IT projects ever succeed. Of course, there are many successful projects which have been both late and significantly over budget. Thus these two criteria alone are not sufficient to indicate success or failure.

Failure is a major problem in IS projects as it is especially costly, not only because of the resources invested, or rather spent on the failed system, but also because such failure frequently causes disruption to the organisation's mode of business.

Furthermore failure can sometimes have serious adverse effects on the morale of the information systems staff and other individuals in the organisation.[1]

1.4   Definition of risk

Risk is a challenging concept to define, understand and ultimately to manage. This is primarily because the idea of risk can mean different things to different people. In terms of a formal definition, risk is described as *the probability that the actual input variables and the outcome results may vary from those originally estimated* (Remenyi *et al.* 1993, Correia *et al.* 1989). This implies that the extent of the possible/probable difference between the actual and expected values reflects the magnitude of the risk.

Another way of looking at the definition of risk is provided by Chapman and Ward (1997) who state that:

A broad definition of project risk is 'the implication of the existence of significant uncertainty about the level of project performance achievable'.

There is always uncertainty about any estimates of IS project development performance, as these estimates attempt to predict how complex work activity will be performed in the future. As the future is always unknown, estimates are always therefore vulnerable to error.

Of course risk is ubiquitous in every aspect of life. Economic theory suggests that risk is at the heart of the economic process and this body of theory suggests there is no profit without some level of risk and that in fact the more risky the investment the higher the profit potential from that investment should be. However Boyadjian and Warren (1987) point out that:

Risky investments may indeed carry a 'premium' reward but the existence of

---

[1] IS failure can cause serious difficulties with respect to the credibility of the IS staff and their ability to function successfully in an organisation. Lack of creditability is often said to be a major obstacle in the successful employment of information systems. As a result of IS project failure, in extreme cases, some line managers believe that there is little or no basis for referring to IS staff as professional. Thus this is a serious problem.

a precise relationship between the two cannot be demonstrated or verified as there is no objective and generally accepted method of evaluating risk.

However, Frank (1987) clarified the relationship between risk and profits quite succinctly when he pointed out that:

Profits are due not to risk, but to superior skill in taking risks. They are not subtracted from the gains of labour but are earned, in the same sense in which the wages of skilled labour are earned.

Although the word risk is usually used in the context of a potential hazard or the possibility of an unfortunate outcome resulting from a given action (Correia et al. 1989), intrinsically risk can be either positive or negative. For example, projects may finish either early or late, or be under or over the financial amounts budgeted. Unfortunately information systems developers sometime neglect the positive side of risk.[2]

1.5 Uncertainty and risk

Sometimes the term uncertainty is also used in connection with projects and investments and thus it is important to note that the terms 'risk' and 'uncertainty', although sometimes used interchangeably, are in fact quite different notions. However, it is true to say that risk is the result of a situation having an uncertain outcome as is inherent in most investment projects. The risk of a project is frequently known and can be measured and managed. Uncertainty on the other hand refers to situations where there is little or even no knowledge of what the outcomes might be.

Correia et al. (1989) state that there is a formal difference between uncertainty and risk. In their definition of these concepts they point out that:

---

[2] IS consultants and academics who generally see risk management as dealing with the down side associated with development problems are often accused of being natural born pessimists. It is indeed most important to be aware of the fact that good project management can deliver the up side potential of being ahead of time, below budget while delivering the required or better functionality.

uncertainty implies that either all the alternative possible outcomes cannot be identified, or that no probability can be attached to the alternative possible outcomes.

Risk on the other hand implies that it is possible to attach probabilities to identified expected outcomes.

For the purpose of this book the authors have focused on the issues related to risk as defined above rather than to uncertainty. In the context of IS development, risk is defined as *the chance that the system will not deliver the planned and expected benefits due to problems encountered during its production.* Thus the concept of risk is directly related to the notion of the chance or probability of particular type of problem arising. The most important feature about the notion of chance is that it relates to future events and thus the issue of risk is entirely to do with what will happen in the future.

1.6   IS project risk management

To be successful, IS project risk management needs to be tackled as a sub-set of IS project management.

IS risk management is a technique that can reduce the possibility, or more correctly the probability, of information system failure, and thus it is essential that it be treated as an integral part of any IS planning activity.[3] This is an important issue, because even a minimal amount of risk management can substantially reduce the probability of costly and inconvenient problems and even IS failures.

---

[3] In fact IS risk management should be seen as a specific sub-set of information systems project planning. Of course planning is not always given as much attention as perhaps it deserves. The business passion for planning frequently only flourishes during periods of either stability or low activity, when there is no great pressure for change or immediate flexibility, or when the organisation is not desperately busy. The same, or a similar point is sometimes made about the state of the tidiness of the desks of employees. Tidy desks are sometimes said to suggest that there is not much going on. A desk piled high with papers and reports is an indication of a busy member of staff who may be achieving a lot and be too occupied to file them.

Formally defined risk management is:

the science and art of recognising the existence of threats, determining their consequences on resources, and applying modifying factors in a cost effective manner to keep adverse consequences within bounds.

(McGaughty 1994)

Although risk management should be focused on during the early stages of the project, when the risks can be identified and risk reduction plans can be put into place, it is in fact an issue which lives throughout the entire life of the project and as such needs continual attention and reassessment.[4]

This is illustrated in Figure 1.1 from which it may be seen that although the main risk identification activity should take place early in the project, i.e. during the feasibility stage, the risk issue is one which demands management attention right through the entire

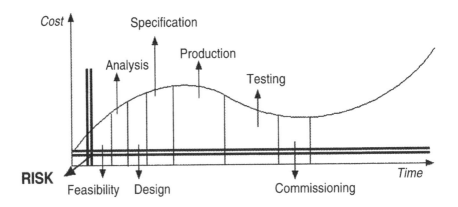

Figure 1.1 Risk is an issue throughout the project life cycle

---

[4] Ideally IS risk management should be initiated during the feasibility stage of the software development life cycle (SDLC) when the project team should conduct an analysis of the risk elements facing the project. If this is done an IS risk management programme may be set in place from the very outset of the development project. However, sometimes this is not done and some IS development projects are commenced without feasibility studies. Even if the work on the development of the project has begun without a risk analysis it is not too late to commence a risk analysis and begin a risk management programme.

project. Thus risks cannot be disposed of quickly, but rather their management needs to be fully integrated into the full range of project management thinking.

It is also important to state that if the risk management process was not commenced during the early stages of the project, this does not mean that risk management is irrelevant. Risk management may be started at any stage of the software development life cycle (SDLC).

Thus the subject of IS risk management is a sub-set of IS project management which deals with the anticipation of problems, quantifying their potential impact and planning to minimise their possible effect on the project. Information systems risk management is an integral part of all project management and should not be seen as a separate issue. Unfortunately this view is not yet well established, at least in part because:

Risk management in technical projects is a relatively new discipline, dating from around 1980. . . . Risk management for software projects has been formalised within the past two years.

(Fairley 1990)

It is believed that this lack of risk assessment and risk management has directly contributed to failure. Thus McFarlan:

. . . partly attributes . . . IS project failures to lack of assessment of individual project risks and the ripple effects such risks can have on a portfolio of projects.

(quoted in Ewusi-Mensha and Przasnyski, 1991)

Furthermore Fairley (1990) states:

Failure to do an adequate job of risk management leaves the outcome of a software project to a matter of luck and unfounded optimism. Systematic risk management provides the framework, viewpoint and techniques needed to replace luck with engineering discipline.

In fact any attempt to involve luck in management is a highly unsatisfactory and perilous exercise. According to Bernstein (1996): *involving luck obscures truth, because it separates an event from its cause.*

Many organisations ignore information systems project risks

Information systems project risk management is either not undertaken at all or is very poorly performed by many if not most organisations. The reason for this is curious as most business professionals are aware of the importance of making sure that their information systems development function operates effectively. One explanation sometimes given is that focusing on potential problems is somehow seen as being negative. Management seems to want to have a more positive attitude towards information systems development. This is in spite of the fact that information systems are famous, or rather infamous, for the frequency with which they are late or have exceeded budget, or have not provided the features or facilities expected of them.

Thus many organisations need to be sensitised to the advantages that can be obtained through effective information systems project risk management. This is clearly a prerequisite before a project risk programme can be successfully implemented.

In fact simple luck is not a dimension on which professional IS development staff can afford to rely.

There is common consensus that project management directly contributes to project success. The way that this occurs is well described by Turner (1993) when he says:

Effective project management aims to reduce risk in two ways, either by developing a project model which, by thorough design and planning, minimizes the inherent uncertainty, or by implementing a project strategy which makes the team better able to respond to deviations as they occur.

As an integral part of the project management discussed by Turner, IS project risk management plays a special role in directly improving the project manager's ability to successfully implement projects despite the uncertainty described above.

1.7 The special nature of information systems

There are a number of special reasons why IS development is so risky. These special reasons, which are itemised below, may be seen as the fundamental circumstances in which IS developments have to occur.

1.7.1 New technology

Information systems are technologically very demanding. There is continuous pressure to advance the technological frontiers by using new processes, new storage devices and by using faster telecommunications rates. There are virtually continuous software developments, both at the application and the systems level. No sooner do IS professionals master an information technology than they are faced with learning to cope with new developments from the laboratories.

1.7.2 Information systems developments are intrinsically cash hungry

High technology always requires extensive capital for development. In addition high technology needs research and development. It needs extensive testing which takes more time and funding. Large-scale improvements in the technology, combined with nearly insatiable markets have tended to push down the unit cost of information technology, especially the unit cost of hardware. The cost of software has also been on the decline, if not in such a dramatic way. Thus although much has been made of the dramatic improvements in the cost–performance ratio of information technology over the past years' it is true to say that organisations have never spent as much money on information systems as they do today.

While hardware and software costs have been on the decline, other costs have not behaved in a similar way. In particular the organisational costs of information technology have been on the increase. This has been for several reasons, including the fact that in recent years' organisations have been undertaking increasingly ambitious applications that have increasingly required extensive organisational change and learning. The cost of these used to be ignored in the past, but is increasingly being considered as part of the price of IS applications. Figure 1.2 reflects the trend in the relative importance of the cost components of information systems. Note that the trend in the increasing importance of organisational cost is likely to continue well into the future.[5]

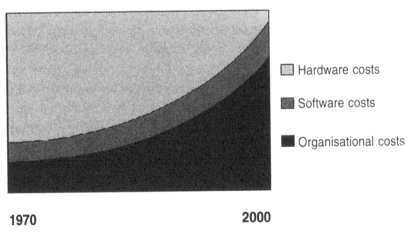

1970   **2000**

Figure 1.2 The relative costs of IS development

1.7.3 The time factor

The development of information systems takes time. Even rapid application development (RAD) approaches do not produce robust, industrial strength systems very quickly. Time is required to understand the business problem or business opportunity. Time is required to develop the systems specification. The production of code is not intrinsically time consuming and in some cases may be automated. However, the testing of programs is a notoriously

[5] Throughout the period from 1970 to today, IS have become more and more complex as organisations have used this technology to tackle increasingly complex problems. This has resulted in the need to re-engineer or to restructure or in some cases, to redefine the organisation. The handling of these highly complex systems accounts for the relatively large increases in the organisational costs.

time-consuming process, and with increasingly large and sophisticated systems, testing has become a difficult issue.

One of the paradoxes associated with software development is that attempts to speed up the SDLC will generally result in lengthening the time required to complete the project. The aphorism, "more haste, less speed" very much applies in the area of information systems.

The London Ambulance Service

The computer press is littered with examples of information technology fiascos or near disasters. An example is the computer-aided dispatch system introduced into the London Ambulance Service in 1992. The £1.5 million system was brought into full use at 07:00 hours on 26 October and almost immediately began to 'lose' ambulances. During that and the next day less than 20% of ambulances reached their destinations within 15 minutes of being summoned, a very poor performance when compared with the 65% arriving within 15 minutes the previous May and the target set by the Government of 95%. The service reverted to semi-computerised methods during the afternoon of 27 October and then right back to manual methods on 4 November when the system locked up altogether and could not be re-booted successfully (South West Regional Health Authority, 1993).

1.7.4   Requires highly skilled people

Partly because hardware and software has been developing so quickly, and partly because organisations have been pushing the potential of information systems to their extremes, highly skilled people are required. These people need constant training and updating.

There has always been a high level of staff turnover in the information systems industry and this trend continues. If anything the demand for highly skilled people has never been greater and the supply just hasn't been able to keep up.

1.7.5   The job is never finished

Increasingly, organisations are coming to realise that the information systems development task is never-ending. No sooner has a system been commissioned, than there is inevitably a need for further development. Often this additional development has been disguised as maintenance, but in reality it has been development of new features and facilities. Furthermore, as the underpinning technology develops so there will be scope for much-improved systems, and as the unit cost of the technology declines so new applications that were previously uneconomical will become financially feasible.

1.8   Successful IS applications do not deliver benefits on their own

Information systems are effectively capital items in the traditional economic theory sense. This means that the value of information systems is intrinsically in the results of their application. In simple terms this means that information systems do not produce benefits in their own right, but rather they are important tools by which business processes and practices can be improved. This improvement is what produces business benefits.

Therefore there is only an indirect relationship between the purchase of, or the investment in, information systems and business benefits. It is because of the poor understanding of this aspect of the nature of IS expenditure that information systems are sometimes seen as just a cash drain, while the benefits are seen as belonging to change or reorganisation champions. Sometime IS people do not get the credit for the valuable contributions they make towards improving organisations' processes and practices.

1.9   IS project risk management and the development environment

The degree to which IS project risk management is important to an organisation is a reflection of the organisation's previous success in delivering effective IS within time and budget constraints. If there has been a history of IS project failure in the organisation, then risk management may be held in greater importance, especially if the projects which failed had not had the benefit of a risk management programme.

On the other hand, if risk management was in place and the project still failed, then there may well be a hostile attitude towards IS project risk management. Understanding the environmental background and making accommodation for attitudes in the organisation due to previous success or failure is an important part of any effective IS project risk programme.

1.10   The key role of perception

As has been emphasised, IS project risk management is a sub-set of IS project management. But it is deceptive. At first glance it appears to be a fairly routine sub-set of IS project management, and indeed it is best understood and implemented as being a part of that process. However it is probably by far the most difficult part of IS project management with a number of sometimes hidden challenges.

The management of IS project risk is essentially an art not a science. There are many difficult cognitive, personal, and political issues involved, some of which are described in Figure 1.3.

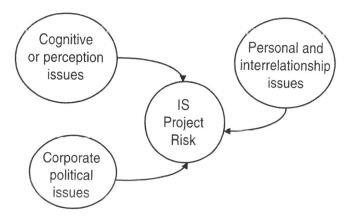

Figure 1.3 The cognitive, personal and political issues involved in IS risk management

As far as cognition is concerned there is first of all the question of how to identify or recognise potential problems which have not yet raised their head above the parapet. Then there is the question of being able to see the probability of these problems occurring increase to the point where action needs to be taken. These cognitive problems are complicated by the personal and interrelationship issues based on the fact that bad news is generally unwelcome. Blowing the whistle on a project is often an unpopular move. To add to these dilemmas there is the question of corporate political issues, which sometimes prevents appropriate action being taken to remedy a deteriorating situation.

Even when risks are recognised and an appropriate assessment is made of their potential impact, the question of how to effect a course of action presents challenges. For example, adequate resources may not be available or there may not be the will to make the changes required to avoid or ameliorate the risk. The problems may be outside the competence or beyond the authority of the IS staff and the other stakeholders may not be prepared to accommodate the changes required to ensure that the project remains within acceptable parameters.

Furthermore, there is always the problem associated with the continuous tension between what is important and what is urgent. IS professionals are frequently optimistic, and management has little time for 'maybe' and 'perhaps' which are at the heart and soul of risk management.

1.11 Summary

Information systems development represents many difficult challenges to most organisations because intrinsically IS developments are difficult, costly and take time. Many organisations do not really recognise these challenges and assume that IS development projects will proceed smoothly or routinely as per plan, without taking adequate cognisance of the possible problems that can occur. It is the role of IS project risk management to recognise possible problems and to make necessary plans to avoid them wherever possible, or where it is not possible to so do, then to minimise their impact. If this is to be done successfully, IS project risk management needs to be seen as an integral part of project management and should be treated as an essential part of any project management activity.

There is little doubt that IS development risk management is a key issue for IS managers who wish to ensure a high level of success in their IS development activities.

Key learning points in this chapter

- ❑ Information systems risk management needs to be an integral part of Information Systems Project Management.

- ❑ Information systems risk management should not be simply seen as a way to avoid potential problems as an emphasis on using it to produce more effective information systems usually produces better results.

- ❑ Information systems risks need to be identified during the feasibility stage and managed throughout the whole life of the project.

- ❑ The general increase in organisational costs experienced by information systems is an important area on which to focus

Practical action guidelines

Review your project management methodology to establish where the risk management process is involved.

If there is no risk management process then either create one or change the project management methodology to include the risk management process.

Look carefully at your financial estimates of the cost of the project to ensure that organisational costs are included. Through discussion with colleagues make sure that a reasonable amount has been allocated for the possible organisational cost of the information system. These organisational costs will include staff learning the new system, staff transfers, new recruitment costs, possible redundancy, changes to pay etc. to compensate staff for new working responsibilities.

2 | What goes wrong with IS development projects

The management of an information systems project risk is often a highly intuitive art.

(Turner, 1993)

Now, there is a law written in the darkest of the Books of Life, and it is this; If you look at a thing nine hundred and ninety-nine times, you are perfectly safe; if you look at it the thousand time, you are in frightful danger of seeing it for the first time.

(Chesterton, 1968)

2.1 Introduction

All sorts of things can go wrong with IS development. The problems range from relatively minor issues such are small hiccups with the hardware and software to complete failure of the system resulting in considerable business damage and loss, such as that which occurred to FoxMeyer, described in Chapter 1. It is actually quite hard to generalise about these problems. They are always contextual and are entirely reliant on the type of information systems being developed, the exact technology solution being used and the individuals involved. In addition, the previous experience the organisation has had with IS projects, including the number of successes and failures which have been experienced in recent years, often determines the approach to risk. Thus according to Willocks and Griffiths (1994):

A history of information systems success or failure seems to have a bearing on subsequent risks experienced.

The previous history of risk is so important that some IS project managers suggest that IS project risk management should begin with an appraisal of the success or failure of all the major projects undertaken by the organisation over the past 12 or even 24 months. Clearly this is a substantial amount of work and would probably only be justified in particularly difficult circumstances.

The list of potential problems is practically endless and any difficulty that could occur, even relatively small ones, can be seen as a risk to the success of an IS development. Thus it is important to introduce IS project risk management as soon as possible in any development project.

A critical aspect of IS risk management is to have a framework for identifying risks and for evaluating the consequences if they actually occur. It is important to have a clear understanding of the drivers or original causes of the risk and what actions the organisation can take to minimise the possibility of these potential problems occurring.

There are at least four important issues to bear in mind when thinking about IS project risks. They vary depending on the:

1 organisation's maturity with regards to its IS function and processes;

2 project type being developed;

3 stage of the project at the time the risk management programme commences, and

4 people involved who may be risk averse, risk tolerant or even risk inclined.

The first step in achieving a clear understanding of how IS project risks behave is to have an appreciation of the maturity level of the IS function within the organisation. This has a direct impact on how information systems are perceived and managed, and the types of risk that may be encountered.

2.2   IS department's maturity cycle and risk

A major factor that affects an organisation's approach to risk and IS risk management is the stage of the IS department's overall maturity (Nolan and Norton, 1968). Well-established IS departments, which usually have a lot of experience, will have a degree of understanding of IS development project risk and will have a track record of ensuring that they can cope with risk exposure. Newer IS departments, on the other hand, may not have had the benefit of these types of experiences. Furthermore, the stage of maturity an department is currently at will affect the types of development risk to which it is exposed. The stages in growth of an IS department from initiation to maturity can be seen in Figure 2.1.

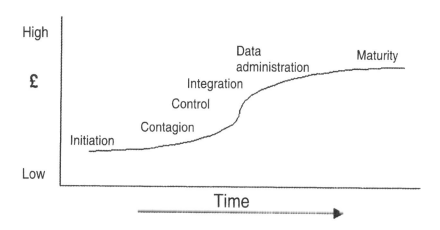

Figure 2.1 Stages of IS growth within an organisation and relative budget expenditures

The major risks that can be encountered at each stage in the development of an IS department are listed in Figure 2.2.

2.2.1   Initiation

When an organisation is in the initiation phase of an IS development, the main IS project risk is related to whether the proposed technological solution will work. By definition, if the

Stages	Issues
Initiation	Will the technology work?
Contagion	Will expenses get out of hand?
Control	Will opportunities be lost?
Integration	Are the right platforms in place?
Data administration	Are we becoming too bureaucratic?
Maturity	Do we understand all the ways IT can support the business?

Figure 2.2 IS Department's maturity cycle and risk

organisation is still in the initiation phase, then its experience with the technology is limited and thus considerable care will have to be taken with hardware and software risks. The main risk will be that of the organisation going off on the wrong track and acquiring inappropriate technology.

Few organisations of any size are still in this stage, although there may occasionally be a department that has just come to understand the advantages of information systems. Consequently, risks involving the acquisition of inappropriate technology are not frequently encountered. Where an organisation is quite new to IS development, they will find it beneficial to employ consultants who can play an important role in reducing the project risk.

2.2.2 Contagion

During the contagion phase of an IS department development the speed with which systems can be delivered tends to be a key issue, and thus care needs to be taken especially when estimating costs and delivery schedules. Unbridled enthusiasm for the technology may blur sensible planning considerations. The main risk will be that of the organisation going overboard and attempting to acquire or achieve too much too quickly.

Careful monitoring of the use of information systems as well as regular reviews of IS related benefits will reduce the risks associated with the contagion stage of IS departmental growth.

2.2.3 Control

As the control phase is characterised by caution, there should be relatively few project management risks during this stage. The main risks are more to do with management considerations related to missing out on sound IS opportunities. Benchmarking can be used to help reorientate the organisation away from excessive or too-strict controls.

2.2.4 Integration

IS integration has always been difficult and many projects have floundered in their attempts to produce sophisticated levels of integration. The main risk here is the possibility of taking on IS projects that are just too big, too difficult or too expensive for the organisation. The risks associated with the integration stage of the development of an IS department may be ameliorated by the production and use of a well conceptualised and articulated IS architecture.[1]

2.2.5 Data administration

In a similar way to control, the data administration phase is concerned with regulation and is thus characterised by caution. The key project management risks are related to understanding the way a particular information system is used in the organisation and how proper data administration procedures can help the organisation get more from the application of the technology. One of the main risks at this stage is that of the organisation going too slowly and becoming too bureaucratic.

---

[1] IS architecture has as its primary objective the establishment of the firm's long-term technology infrastructure which will allow systems to be designed and implemented in an effective and efficient way. The architecture seeks to avoid, *inter alia*, fragmentation, redundancy and inconsistency. It defines components, formats, structure, and interfaces. The importance with which the architecture is regarded is often seen as a measure of the firm's IT status, direction and strategy. An IS architecture is an important step in ensuring that all the key stakeholders in the organisation understand how information systems can be used to enhance the firm's ability to achieve its objectives.

This type of risk may be minimised by achieving a high level of IS understanding within the organisation. This understanding needs to focus on how information systems can support the real business issues and how it can effect material improvements to organisational processes and practices.

2.2.6 Maturity

As the technology is still so relatively new,[2] it is generally believed that organisations have yet to reach the maturity phase in the development cycle. In fact with the speed of developments in hardware, software and IS management, it could be argued that the maturity phase will never be reached. As soon as an organisation appears to be reaching a stable position with regards to its use of information technology, a new development will cause the demand of the technology to be stimulated and the organisation will effectively be relaunched on a new technology absorption curve.

However, the more mature the IS department, the more likely it is to recognise IS development risk, and to instigate appropriate risk management procedures. Thus where this stage has been reached the risks are likely to be low.

2.3 Risk and the nature of IS projects

Besides the issues of the IS department's maturity cycle, there are several other important issues which need to be considered when reflecting on the risk of a project. McFarlan (1990) suggests that the actual size of the project is a major risk. In simple terms a project with a budget of £100 million is, all other things being equal, intrinsically more risky than a project with a £10 million or even a £50 million budget. There can however, be exceptions to this proposition.

---

[2] Business computing or information systems may be regarded to have begun no earlier than the 1950s, although many would argue that it did not really take off until the 1960s. However a systematic approach to IS management really only began on any substantial scale somewhat later.

In addition to size, the planned duration of the project is a directly associated variable and is another major risk issue. In general the longer the possible duration of the IS project the greater the risk. The realisation of this has placed considerable importance on techniques such as rapid application development (RAD) and joint application development (JAD) in order to speed up the process.

There are two other main causes of risk, which McFarlan describes as risks associated with failures of execution and risks caused by failures of conceptualisation.

2.3.1 Risk associated with failures of execution

The risks associated with failures of execution can be derived from two sources:

1 the structuredness of a project, and

2 the degree to which a project incorporates company-familiar technology.

The structuredness of an IS project may be defined as the extent to which the project is fully understood and the detail agreed to by the major stakeholders. Routine IS applications such as those required for the payroll function are generally regarded as being highly structured. Applications such as EDI or MRP II, which for many organisations break new ground and require close collaboration between a number of internal and external stakeholders, are regarded as having a low degree of structure.

The degree to which a project incorporates company-familiar technology refers to how little or how much experience the organisation has had with the specific technology. Clearly, leading-edge technology can turn into very expensive and damaging bleeding-edge problems, and risk management needs to be employed to prevent this happening.

A 2-by-2 matrix can be helpful in positioning the different levels of risk relative to the dimensions of structuredness of the project and novelty of the technology, see Figure 2.3.

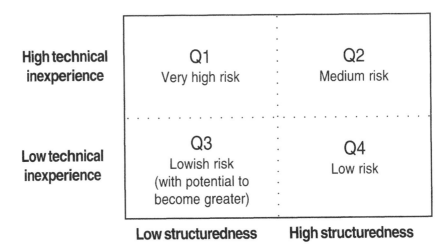

Figure 2.3 Matrix showing different degrees of risk (source: McFarlan 1990)

It is useful to consider each of the four quadrants in the figure separately.

2.3.2 Quadrant 1 (Q1) – very high risk

In Quadrant 1 the project has low structuredness and makes extensive use of technology that is new to the organisation. These projects are fundamentally difficult. Projects in this category should be considered by the organisation to be extremely high-risk projects. Project managers with both technical and people skills are required to make them work. PERT charts and other project management monitoring techniques simply infer the project's direction, but are otherwise not especially useful in establishing its time position. McFarlan asserts that these projects are "not done until they are done!" Managers of them would expect numerous and frequent mid-stream changes. They are always very expensive and their expense is derived primarily from the changes that are inevitably made to the original and even to subsequently modified specifications. Both a high degree of technical, project management and business process experience will be required from the project manager and the IS champion if this type of information system is to succeed.

The source of the greatest risk?

The McFarlan analysis described here suggests that when it come to risks of execution, the novelty of the technology provides the greatest source of risk to an IS development project. Although the difficulties associated with new technology should never be underestimated, it is probably true to say that in general the technology is increasingly less problematical. The real problems are now, and are likely to be in the future, directly related to the increasingly complex projects and processes to which information systems solutions are being applied.

2.3.3   Quadrant 2 (Q2) – medium risk

In Quadrant 2 the project makes use of technology which is new to the organisation but also has a high degree of structuredness. These projects are nowhere near as difficult as projects in Quadrant 1.

Projects such as these are generally regarded to be of medium risk. It is usual to expect mid-stream corrections with them. PERT charts and other project management monitoring techniques offer a fair representation of project status, but should not be totally relied upon. Implications of the new technology that were not originally understood by the organisation may upset production plans and cause developers to have to re-do some of the items in the SDLC. It is suggested that managers who are highly technically competent be closely involved in the steering of projects of this type.

2.3.4   Quadrant 3 (Q3) – lowish (with potential to become greater) risk

In Quadrant 3 the project has a low degree of structuredness and does not use technology which is new to the organisation. These projects are relatively low risk, but with potentially hidden problems. Many of them fail when really they should succeed relatively easily. To ensure success in these projects, it is important that a strong and highly assertive user-manager be placed in control, or at least a high level of user involvement be sought throughout their duration. It is important to emphasise that this should not only be at the outset of the project, but on a continuous basis for the purpose of on-going verification that the project deliverables are still relevant. The problem of risk with this class of project is the potential mid-stream change requests. Strict parameters need to be constructed around the project otherwise a continuous stream of change-requests from users will arise and the project will in all likelihood flounder and fail. The PERT chart and other project management monitoring techniques offer managers a succinct view for these projects, but should be only utilised if a strong project manager can in some way incorporate a degree of structuredness.

2.3.5 Quadrant 4 (Q4) – low risk

In Quadrant 4 the project has highly specified outcomes and outputs and low use of technology that is new to the organisation. There should be no major difficult with this type. These are low risk projects due to the tight definition of expected outputs and the use of familiar technology. As a result of the low risk level, companies can assign new or relatively inexperienced project managers to them. The use of PERT charts and other project management monitoring techniques provide accurate indications of the completeness of the work. Due to the constricted nature of the outputs, minimal user involvement is necessary after the project commences. The low-risk profile of these projects means that they should be successful with little need for risk management.

2.3.6 Matching these risk with management approaches

From the above it is clear that different types of projects have different types of implementation risk and, that different projects need different project management approaches if they are to be successful. The project management approach should flow from the project and not the other way around. Figure 2.4 indicates the management approaches that should be applied to different risk profiles described in the McFarlan analysis.

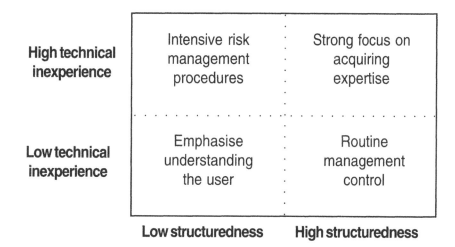

Figure 2.4 Management approaches to projects with different risk profiles

From Figure 2.4 it may be seen that the very high risk described in Quadrant 1 clearly require intensive risk management procedures if the project is not to fail, while the low risk which are typical of Quadrant 4 need no more than routine IS risk management controls.

Additional ideas about how these different types of projects should be handled are supplied in Figure 2.5, which indicates the level of management activity that is required for different risk profiles.

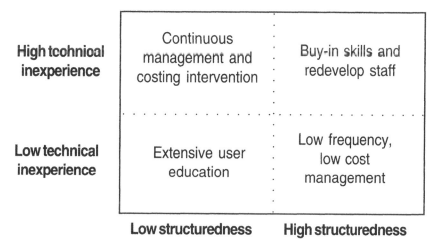

Figure 2.5 Management activity required with different risk profiles

2.3.7 Risks associated with failures of conceptualisation

Failures of conceptualisation are ideas that were not likely to succeed from the beginning, in the sense that they were not sound business ideas. McFarlan (1994), who is especially interested in the concept of obtaining strategic or competitive advantages from IS, identifies the following categories of projects that are likely to fail due to poor conceptualisation:

1 A project that fails to meet a customer's need, no matter how technically sophisticated or perfect it is, is destined to fail. Technology can perform wonders, but if there is no market for the product or service, the project will fail. The original home shopping systems, which dramatically failed, are examples of this type of error.

2 The intended system may require behaviour that is not ingrained in existing users, such as the use of terminals. As people shy away from change, such a system will fail. The early home banking systems are good examples of this type of error.

3 Projects that are easy to replicate will also fail, as competition thrives on timely duplication of simple innovative ideas. The automatic tellers machines (ATM) which appeared to offer a competitive advantage but within a few years had become a sine qua none for any retail banker.

4 Systems incapable of evolving will fail. Evolution is an essential aspect of survival in the dynamic business environment of the

---

Failures of conceptualisation

Poor ideas are almost impossible to recognise in advance. The only protection that we can really provide ourselves from our own potential folly is to avoid the *BIG PROJECT*.

Phased conceptualisation and delivery is a helpful approach to avoiding failures of conceptualisation. There should also be an early warning system in place that can indicate problems before they get out of control.

modern commercial world. All the internationally famous examples of strategic information systems have evolved from relatively simple transaction-based systems.

5   If the system is highly interoperable with other systems, users may see it as a commodity and swap to the cheapest vendor. Hence there is definitely a place for proprietary systems in the modern business environment.

6   Technology can be a double-edged sword, lowering entry barriers by reducing the costs of competing. If the project's ideas are rejected by the customer's culture then it will fail.

7   Projects that are undertaken before all the strategic pieces are in place are going to fail. Set up the alliances that are necessary before undertaking the project.

2.3.8   Matching these risks with management approaches

These failures of conceptualisation involve either a misunderstanding of the client's needs and requirements or a misunderstanding of the technology. These two dimensions can be summarised onto a two-by-two matrix, which is shown in Figure 2.6.

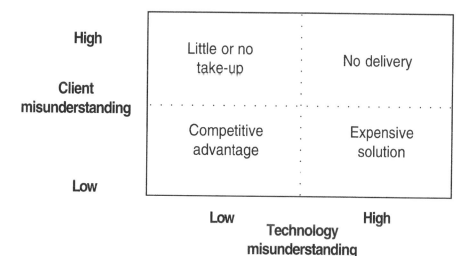

Figure 2.6 Summary of failures of conceptualisation

The McFarlan approach described here is useful as a framework for thinking about risk and information systems. However it is very difficult to detect in advance, errors of conceptualisation. What looks like a great idea may easily flop, perhaps due to the fact that it was simply ahead of its time. On the other hand, ideas which appear to be very unlikely to succeed may sometimes be winners.

2.4 The systems development life cycle and its risks

One of the key contextual issues which needs to be considered when reviewing the risk of an IS development project is the phase at which the project is in the SDLC. This can be an important determinant of the risks the project faces.

2.4.1 SDLC and risk

Problems can occur with IS project developments at any time during the SDLC, and each stage of any project offers its own challenges and problems.

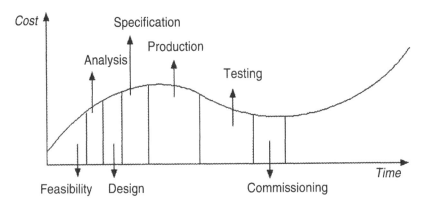

Figure 2.7 Systems developing life cycle (SDLC)

Using the typical SDLC, different primary risks can be identified for each stage. These are illustrated in Figure 2.7.

Some of the key risks that need to be considered at each stage in the SDLC are shown in Figure 2.8.

Stage	Risk
Feasibility	Misunderstanding of the nature of problems, opportunities or technology and the poor estimation of benefits and costs.
Analysis	Lack of understanding as to the detailed activities required to provide a solution.
Design	Misinterpretation of the work done during the analysis or faulty analysis.
Specification	Incomplete work. Previous errors in analysis and design.
Production	Inappropriate development tools. Bugs in the development tools. Staff do not know how to use the tools adequately.
Testing	The system is too big to adequately test in a timeframe that is perceived as being appropriate. Inappropriate test data or routines used.
Commissioning	Not enough attention given by users. Done too fast.

Figure 2.8 SDLC and the key risks

2.5 Feasibility

During the feasibility study of the software development project the key risk is the degree to which the organisation understands the business problem or the business opportunity they face. There is also the possibility that the organisation will misunderstand the technology they intend to employ. There is also the question of whether the intended owners of the proposed information system actually believe that it will improve the process or business practice for which it is intended.

Feasibility studies have been, and perhaps still are, notorious for understating costs. It has been frequently said that if the 'real' costs of an information system were fairly stated in advance, then very few of these projects would obtain management approval. Consequently costs are sometimes understated. When this happens budget reviews are required to supply more funding as the 'real' costs become apparent. This phenomenon is sometimes referred to as the *creeping commitment* approach to IS development. The growth of outsourcing development providers puts added strain on in-house cost estimates.

Changing risks

The fact that risks may change considerably as the project progresses can often be perplexing to IS developers. The major consequence of this phenomenon is that the IS project risk officer's job is never done until the project is fully commissioned. Even then one could argue that the risk remains but in a different form.

2.5.1   Analysis

At the time of analysis the main risk is that the analysts will have a lack of understanding of the detailed activities required to provide a solution to the problem or opportunity being studied. Any errors made at this stage will of course have a knock-on or ripple effect on the remaining phases of the SDLC.

2.5.2   Design

During the design stage the main risk is that the design analysts will misinterpret the work done during the systems analysis phase or that the design analysis will have a faulty or incomplete understanding of the issues related to information systems design.

2.5.3   Specification

The main problems that are encountered during the specification phase relate to incomplete work or incompetence, or to the carrying over of errors which have been previously made during the analysis and design phases.

2.5.4   Production

The term production includes all the activities involved in producing the program code. Sometimes this activity may be automated by the use of code generators. However there is still a large amount of manual or human coding undertaken. The risks here are to do with the programmer not understanding the computer language, the computer operating system, the limitations of the hardware or the communications aspects of the system, etc.

2.5.5 Testing

Increasingly competent and comprehensive testing has become a significant problem that often carries with it a high risk. It is difficult to test large sophisticated systems. There are, in some cases, countless numbers of permutations of events that could occur and for which there needs to be a test. Testing is time consuming and really quite expensive. Software suppliers sometimes try to use their potential clients to help with the testing by providing them with alpha or beta test versions.

2.5.6 Commissioning

Problems encountered during the commissioning phase relate to not having the organisation and the people adequately prepared for the new system.

2.5.7 Feasibility: summary

It is clear from the above that the risk profile faced by a project changes throughout the project's SDLC and thus risk management needs to be maintained from the very start of the project until it is finally commissioned. Thus in preparing a risk management plan IS management needs to assess the risks on a continuous basis from the start of the project to the end.

2.6 Detailed problems

The generic level or types of risks described above can lead to many different problematical outcomes. In fact it could be said that there are at least ten IS implementation problems which may be the result of these risks and these are listed in Figure 2.9.

It will never be delivered	It will be delivered late
It will exceed its budget	It will lack functionality
It will contain errors	It will not be usable
The IS will fail during operation	It will be too difficult to enhance
It will be too costly to support	It will not perform to required standards

Figure 2.9 Some of the risks associated with an IS project

It is these types of problems or challenges the IS manager or the IS project manager will have to face if the risk actually materialises and is not rectified or ameliorated.

Although the above table is not definitive, it provides an indication of the types of outcomes an organisation can face when implementing a new information system. It is crucial that the organisation identifies and manages all of the risks associated with a potential project so as to increase the chances of success. The organisation thus needs to instigate a risk management process that encompasses the identification, evaluation and control of the IS risks being faced in order to minimise the losses that could adversely affect it as a result of systems development activities going wrong (Berny and Townsend 1993).

2.7   Summary

IS departments and the way they are managed differ for many reasons. IS project risk profiles depend on a large number of variables and these need to be carefully researched and studied if successful IS risk management is to be implemented.

Furthermore the course of action required to reduce or remove the risk will also be very context dependent.

Some of the important reasons why IS project risks differ relate to organisational history, the location of IS department's in the maturity cycle, the nature of the IS project itself and its position in the SDLC.

Key learning points in this chapter

- ❑ The organisation's attitude towards IS Risk management depends upon, *inter alia*, its history of project success and failure. Thus it is important for you as an IS Risk Manager to know your organisation's track record in this respect.

- ❑ The maturity level of the IS Department will directly affect the types of risks a project may face.

- ❑ IS risk management needs to be responsive to the different activities involved at different stages of the SDLC.

- ❑ All IS projects face risks that are derived from failures of execution and failures of conceptualisation. Failures of execution are to do with the structuredness of the IS project and novelty of the technology. Failures of conceptualisation are to do with the information systems not being based on sound business ideas.

Practical action guidelines

Create a risk overview for your proposed projects.

The four practical steps required are:

1 Spend the time to get to know the organisation's track record in IS project development. Understand what success and failures it has recently had and why success has been achieved or failure occurred.

2 Understand where your IS department is in terms of the maturity model.

3 Establish a view on the risk inherent in the nature of the specific IS project being proposed.

4 Establish exactly where the project is in terms of the SDLC and pay particular attention to the major risks for this stage of the project.

3 | Risk, control and time

Our knowledge of the factors which will govern the yield of an investment some years hence is usually very slight and often negligible. If we speak frankly, we have to admit that our basis of knowledge for estimating the yield ten years hence of a railway, a copper mine, a textile factory, the goodwill of a patent medicine, an Atlantic liner, a building in the City of London amounts to little and sometimes to nothing; or even five years hence.

(Keynes, 1964)

3.1 Introduction

There are three key risk management issues which need to be carefully considered at the outset of any IS development project. An assessment of these is vital to the development of a risk management plan. These issues are control, cost and time. They are of fundamental importance to how the risk of any particular IS project will be managed and thus need to be considered at the outset of any risk planning initiative. IS risk management is an intervention in an IS development project that will provide the project manager with greater control, but it will cost money and it does take up valuable time. There is always a trade-off between these three variables.

3.2 Control and cost

Control and cost are two complementary issues that frequently need to be considered together. Control of the future, as needs to be exercised in the IS development environment, is not easy and where it is possible, it can often be expensive. Thus, there are distinct trade-offs between the cost of control of an IS development project and the acceptable level of risk. It should be noted that the control mechanisms necessary to keep the risks in check are not one-off events, but will be required throughout the SDLC.

3.2.1 A rolling ball metaphor

A useful way of envisioning the risk element associated with IS development is to consider the three dimensional space described in Figure 3.1. This diagram considers the problem involved in rolling a ball from the point marked X to the point marked Y. The three-dimensional space in the figure attempts to show what may be thought of as a large sheet of rubber with a significant fold in the near side. If the ball rolls directly from point X to Y it will have to traverse over the fold, which because of its height may cause the ball to bounce off the sheet and fall away on to the floor. But there are a number of ways of moving the ball from X to Y without having to proceed directly over the large drop that the fold represents.

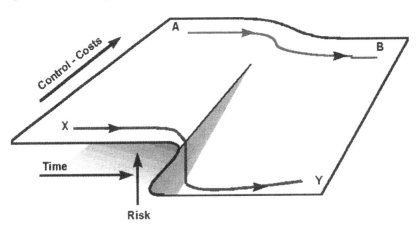

Figure 3.1 The three dimensions of the concept of project risk

If the ball can somehow be moved from point X to point A, then from point A to point B and subsequently from point B to Y, the ball may be positioned at the required point without having to travel over the deep fold in the sheet. This is demonstrated in Figure 3.2.

Using this analogy it may be noted that the depth of the fold represents the risk of the project. The distance the ball has to travel from point X to point A represents the control which is placed on the situation in order to reduce the risk and could be measured in terms of resources or even money. Notice the journey from A to B is

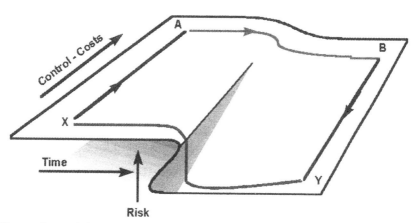

Figure 3.2 Deliberately avoiding project risks

not entirely smooth as no project is totally risk free, but the deep fold has been replaced by a relatively small wrinkle in the surface. The wrinkle between A and B represents a much reduced risk. The distance from X to Y is the development activity that takes place over time.

The above analogy suggests that there are multiple routes or ways in which a project can proceed and that the risk associated with the project may be controlled, provided resources are expended on its management. It is always a challenging task to balance the cost of control with the required reduction in risk (Turner, 1993).

3.2.2 Risk entropy

In concluding the rolling ball metaphor, it is important to note the existence of risk entropy. According to the Merriam-Webster's Collegiate Dictionary, entropy is a measure of the system's disorder. In the context of IS risk management a project's risk entropy refers to its tendency to follow the route outlined in Figure 3.3 by the AZB line. This route does not follow the AB path where the risk profile is relatively low, but takes the project down to the high risk point, Z. In other words, without strict IS risk management, problems will creep in and the course of a project will tend towards the route of the greatest risk.

The Murphy's Law of information systems

Risk entropy may be seen as the equivalent concept of the Murphy's Law of IS development. If projects are not properly managed with due regard to risk issues then they are likely to encounter problems and be late and /or over budget or even fail completely.

It is because of risk entropy that IS risk management has to be an on-going or continuous affair. It is not enough to identify the risk at the feasibility stage of the project and to then simply put risk management processes in place.

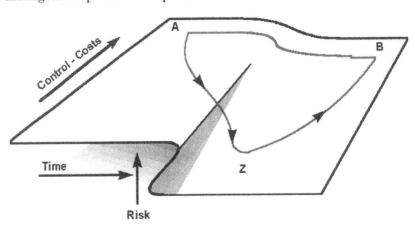

Figure 3.3 Risk entropy

IS risk management requires continual auditing to ensure that the project has not inadvertently rolled off the required route or course. Thus regular risk auditing is an essential part of any IS risk management process.

3.3 The time, information and risk equation

The dimensions, from the point of view of size, of the risks a project faces may be seen as a function of the amount of information available to the project planners at the time the project is initiated. As the planners acquire more information about the project so the risks become apparent, can be understood, and the possibility of controlling and reducing them increases. This is demonstrated by the *information reducing risk* line in Figure 3.4 and is vividly expressed by Bernstein (1996) when he said:

Yet once we act, we forfeit the option of waiting until new information comes along. As a result, not acting has value. The more uncertain the outcome, the greater may be the value of procrastination. Hamlet had it wrong: he who hesitates is halfway home.

However for projects that have a time restraint, which applies to most if not all projects, the risk of the project will increase if it is not promptly commenced. This situation is represented by the *time increasing risk* line, i.e. this is the risk of not completing the project on time. Thus one aspect of risk management may be improved over time while another aspect of the project will normally see the risk increase over time. The overall risk of the project is the sum of these two sub-risks. The project risk profile line in Figure 3.4 reflects this situation, which is the sum of the two sub-risks.

It should be noted that the *project risk profile* line is a U-shaped curve, which suggests that there is an optimal time for action to be taken. Up until the minimum point on the *project risk profile* line the project will benefit from delay when more information is gathered which allows the project manager to better understand the situation. However after the minimum point on the *project risk profile* line the situation changes and any further delay increases the overall project risk.

The analysis shown in Figure 3.4 does not imply that the collection of information about the project or its risks should stop at the point where the project commences. Information collection and risk analysis needs to continue right through the life of the project.

The objective of the project manager is to minimise the risks which the project faces and one of the ways of achieving this is to ensure that there is the maximum acquisition of information consistent with there being sufficient time to complete the project.

3.3 The time, information and risk equation

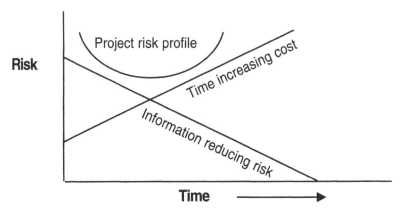

Figure 3.4 The risk and time equation

In practice this means that the project manager needs to shift the *information reducing risk* line, making it as steep as possible. The steeper the learning curve the sooner the project will be able to start.

The slope of the *time increasing risk* line may be flattened by undertaking actions at the start which tend to reduce generic project risks, i.e. infrastructure issues. This can be seen in the adjusted risk and time equation in Figure 3.5.

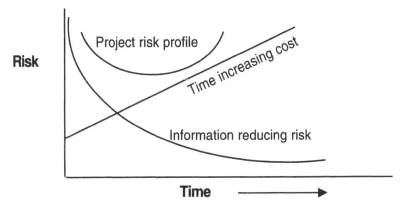

Figure 3.5 The adjusted risk and time equation

3.4 The risk efficiency boundary

In order to put the issues of cost time and risk management into context it is useful to consider the risk efficiency boundary in Figure 3.6. The risk efficiency boundary is an isoquant[1] that shows different solutions to a problem, such as different project management plans that have different cost/time implications as well as different levels of risk. Any point on the isoquant line ABC represents a feasible project plan, which will produce an outcome that will satisfy the organisation's objectives. Point A has a low cost/time profile but has a very high risk. Point C has a very low risk profile but will take much time and will consume a high degree of costs. A point such as D will not be satisfactory as it will be both too costly as well have a too high a level of risk associated with it.

The optimal point on this curve depends upon the organisation's attitude towards risk and cost/time. If the organisation is extremely risk adverse it will chose point C for its project. Thus cost and time will be sacrificed for the sake of lowering the project risks. On the other hand if the organisation is risk inclined and the risk takers want to try to minimise the cost and time implication of the project they will chose to operate at point C.

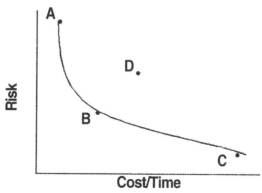

Figure 3.6 The risk and costs/time isoquant

---

[1] An isoquant is a line showing things of the same value, used mostly by economists.

For many organisations point B could be considered to be an optimal solution for this project as it is at this position that risk and cost/time are somewhat in balance.

However, in general all points on the isoquant curve above point B have relatively high-risk profiles and all points below point B have generally low-risk profiles.

The isoquant curve demonstrates that there is an optimal IS risk management approach which is achieved by managing the IS project at point B. Any other point on the curve is either too risky or has excessive cost/time implications. Any point on the graph not on the isoquant curve will not achieve the IS project objectives.

Risk averse

Although most people and many organisations are risk averse it is not true to say that everyone is. Some individuals and organisations look for situations that are regarded as risky as it is generally believed that risk and profit potential go hand in hand. These risk takers are frequently entrepreneurs.

When this notion of risk adverse or risk tolerant or inclined is translated into the IS development environment it is important to understand that the positive attitude towards risk is only to do with the entrepreneurial basis of the change which the information systems will be helping to support. It would not make sense to be risk inclined towards the hardware or the software or any other technical aspect of the project.

Note there are at least three different attitudes towards risk. The position of risk averse is by far the most common when risk is regarded as being equivalent to some sort of "badness". Risk tolerant is the neutral position where risk is neither good or bad. On the other hand risk inclined is the position when the positive profit potential side of the risk equation is seen.

However some organisations that are especially risk adverse will try to move the IS project to a position between point B and point C. It is clear from Figure 3.6 that this is an expensive exercise and before undertaking such a reorientation of the project a careful cost justification should be performed.

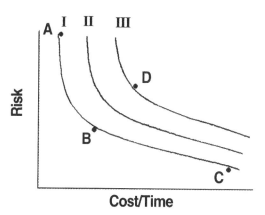

Figure 3.7 The risk and costs/time isoquant

Figure 3.7 shows that there are frequently a series of different isoquants. Isoquant I has the optimal configuration in terms of risk and cost/time. Both isoquant II and III are too risky and have too great a cost/time implication. Isoquants II and III may be using a different type of technology or perhaps a different approach to funding and/or management the IS project.

3.5   Summary

With sufficient control and accompanying funds to implement them, the risks inherent in most IS projects can be very substantially minimised. In fact ,with enough control and funds, risk can almost be eliminated, but never entirely. Risk entropy is always present, even with the best-laid plans. The time, information and risk equation are important aspects of risk management for any IS development project. As IS projects are nearly always time-constrained it is important to ensure that they start in good time, but also that there is adequate information available to appropriately plan.

The risk efficiency boundary shows that it is not optimal to try to reduce the risks of a project beyond a certain point, as there will be a disproportional increase in cost and time.

Key learning points in this chapter

- ☐ IS risk management requires a clear understanding between risk and cost/time variables.

- ☐ Risk may be substantially reduced if enough money is spent and enough time is taken to control it.

- ☐ The more information which the IS project manager has at his or her disposal, the more likely risks can be controlled. Thus projects should only be commenced when enough research has been completed.

- ☐ Isoquants may be used to demonstrate the risk efficiency boundary. This shows that although risk can be substantially reduced, it is not worth pushing the risk down below the point where the risk efficiency boundary is optimal.

Practical action guidelines

Discuss with colleagues involved with the IS project how risk averse your organisation is.

How much extra money would normally be added to an IS project's budget in order to reduce the risk? And how big a reduction of the risk would be required for different levels of expenditure?

Questions to ask include:

Would it be worth spending 2% of the project cost on research in order to understand the problem or opportunity better?

Should we spend another £20,000 a year on a project quality control officer in order to ensure that the IS project risk profile is reduced?

Can we delay the commencement date of the project by another month until all the primary stakeholders have signed off on their acceptance of the outcomes of the projects.

4 The major risks

Real problems are hard to spot, especially for managers so involved in day-to-day operations that they have inadequate perspective to see the big picture.

(Wiersema, 1996)

The world we have made as a result of the level of thinking we have done thus far, creates problems we cannot solve on the same level of thinking at which we created them

(Einstein, 1934)

4.1 Introduction

This chapter discusses from a high-level point of view the actual risk an IS project may have to face. As mentioned in earlier chapters there are many different ways in which a project can go wrong. There are also many different ways of describing or categorising the risks faced by IS project developers. Sometimes, as part of IS risk management, consultants produce long lists of detailed risks which a project could face. These lists sometimes run into dozens of pages. It is sometimes said "beware of long lists of options or possibilities", as they tend to dilute one's focus rather than inform. It has been decided not to address this amount of detail in this book, but to rather discuss generic or major risk categories and to allow the reader to expand these generic risk groups to the appropriate amount of detail for his or her IS project. If the generic or high-level risks are properly understood it is not difficult to add the required amount of detail.

It is useful to consider risk in terms of three major groups or categories. These are business risks, development risks and architecture risks. For each of these categories three individual risks are discussed. However in practice these risks may not balance out numerically in this way. On occasions there may only be one or two business risks, perhaps a dozen development risks and only one or two architecture risks, while on other occasions there may be seven or eight business risks and few development and architecture risks.

4.2 Risk categories: Business, Development and Architecture

In Figure 4.1 the three major risk categories are represented by a jigsaw metaphor. The jigsaw is appropriate because it suggests the interlocking nature of these issues both horizontally within a risk category and vertically across domains or perspectives. Single IS development risks seldom occur. Thus it is important when thinking about IS development risks not to isolate or exaggerate any one risk, as the components of one category of risk will invariably affect another category.

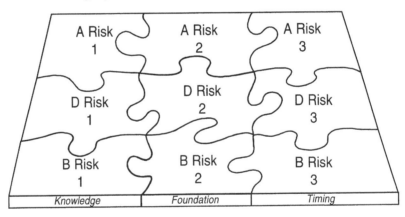

Figure 4.1 The major risk jigsaw. Note: the approximate equal size of the pieces in the above jigsaw does not suggest all the risks described here are likely to be of the same magnitude or importance.

Although there may be any number of risks within a particular category, the three most important risks are discussed here. There are obviously more than three risks facing an IS project under each of these general areas. However it has been decided to focus on the three most serious potential problems which can be encountered. Of course what is considered to be a potentially serious problem is a function of an organisation's culture and its historic experience, but the three mentioned here would be considered to be serious in all organisations (Willocks and Griffiths, 1994).

The order of the risks within the jigsaw in Figure 4.1 is important. The most basic risks, which can easily destroy a project, and which it is quite possible for an organisation not to be fully aware of, are the business risks. Thus these are the most dangerous or difficult challenges facing an IS development project.

Development risks are usually considered the second most problematic, but they tend not to be as devastating to the project as the business risks.

Although still important, architecture risks are, at least in some senses, increasingly less threatening. This is not to say that an IS project cannot be wrecked by poor architecture decisions, but the technology at the turn of the century is more stable and reliable than ever before, and thus it is generally less problematical.

4.3 Business risks

Three key or central business risks have been identified and are illustrated in Figure 4.2. When these risks occur the IS project may totally fail. Later in the book checklists are supplied which provide more detail of the individual risks that could be grouped under the following three headings.

4.3.1 Business risk 1 - Understanding

Business risks are ubiquitous. Many IS projects run into trouble because the business issues have not been correctly understood. Thus the single biggest risk faced by any IS development project is that the main stakeholders have an incomplete or inadequate understanding of the main business problem or opportunity.

The greater the number of important individual stakeholders or groups of stakeholders and the bigger the IS development project,

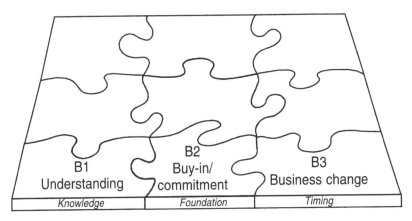

Figure 4.2 Key business risks

however measured, the more likely this risk is to occur. It is clear that without an appropriate understanding,[1] the whole project will probably be on the wrong track. When this happens the IS project cannot deliver any benefits and it usually is abandoned either after it is completed or sometime before. Sometimes insufficient business research is done. IS and business professionals are not fully involved in providing business solutions. Business thinking has been blunted and business concerns are not the central issues for the project.

Business changes

The current way of doing business is characterised by rapid changes to business conditions as well as general business opportunities. For this reason alone substantial business risks are always present and need the considerable attention of both IS and line managers. Without careful focus on the business risks, an IS development project has a very high probability of not being satisfactory.

---

[1] A question often raised is who needs this comprehensive understanding of the IS project? There are at the very least three individuals who have to understand the issues in detail. There are the project sponsor, the project champion and the project manager.)

4.3.2   Business risk 2 – Buy-in/Commitment

Despite initial appearances users don't properly buy-into, or commit to the proposed information system.

Information systems can change the competitiveness of the organisation, they can change the basic strategic focus of the organisation; they can change the efficiency of the organisation; they can change the supply-chain relationships and they can change internal organisation competence and employment factors. In short information systems may radically change businesses at a fundamental level. Therefore if the users haven't bought into the system, and they are not committed to making the business changes necessary to ensuring that the IS project is a success, the project will be very severely compromised. Users who believe that the project was not their idea, or who feel that the new system is being imposed on them, seldom co-operate fully with the IS project. Furthermore, the greater the number of stakeholders the more difficult it is to keep them all committed.

IS projects such as infrastructure investments, which are largely owned by the IS department are usually seen as high risk. Although these are technical projects, which sometimes do not have immediate business benefits, it is nonetheless important that they have business sponsors, business champions and business project managers. This is the only way of ensuring some business buy-in.

4.3.3   Business risk 3 - Changes

Changes that occur to the information system's requirements during development are not accepted or are not accommodated by the IS development project.

Traditionally changes have been seen as the result of something going wrong. In fact changes are frequently an indication that the business is growing and developing. Although it is true that the bigger the project the more difficult it can be to accommodate changes, it is important to ensure that all IS development projects are managed in such a way that they are able to accommodate change when it is needed.[2]

4.4 Development risks

Three key high-level development risks have been identified and are illustrated in Figure 4.3. Although when these risks occur it is unlikely the IS project will totally fail, they can be very disruptive and cause substantial delays and large cost over-runs.

4.4.1 Development risk 1 – Estimating and planning

Estimates of the work required for an IS development project have always been a problem. Estimates of the amount of work required have often been unrealistic. The initial work undertaken during the feasibility, and/or the analysis, and/or the design, and/or the specification stages of the project was inadequate or just simply incorrect.

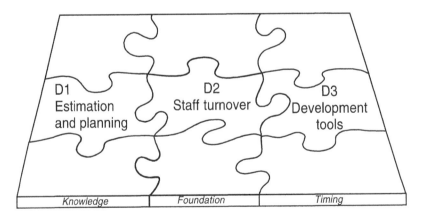

Figure 4.3 Key development risks

---

[2] Allowing changes to IS projects is feared by IS managers because of the issue of scope-creep. Scope-creep refers to an IS development project becoming bigger and bigger when additional requirements surface as a result of the discussion and design phase of the project.

4.4.2 Development risk 2 – Staff turnover

The implementers do not remain in post and/or key users move positions. Although no one is indispensable, when senior project people leave or are transferred the development project will almost inevitably suffer a major setback which can materially delay the delivery of the information systems. As previously mentioned, successful information systems need highly skilled staff and these are nearly always in short supply. On top of this is the question of the learning curve needed by new individuals in order to become familiar with the details of the project.

But perhaps even more important than losing key implementers is the change in the principal stakeholders. When key user/owners change, the whole emphasis of the development project may alter.

4.4.3 Development risk 3 - Development tools

Hardware and software development tools are inappropriate or inadequate or just do not work. There have been many examples of tools that have either been over-hyped and thus did not perform to expectation, or tools that did not perform at all. Despite great expectations for computer-aided systems engineering (CASE) tools they have just not delivered their once suggested and believed potential.

Similarly early versions of object-oriented tools were poorly supported, unable to run on the different platforms which were promised as well have having bugs.

4.5 Architecture risks

Three important or high-level architecture risks have been identified and are illustrated in Figure 4.4. When these materialise they can be very problematical, but in general are unlikely to cause the IS project to totally fail.

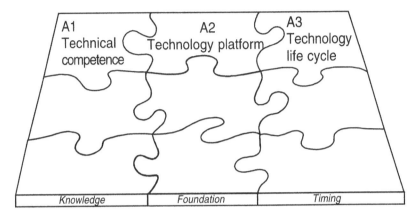

Figure 4.4 Key architecture risks

4.5.1 Architecture risk 1 – Technical competencies

The organisation does not have appropriate expertise to be able to successfully implement the chosen technology.

Some organisations appear to assume that IS people have almost limitless flexibility. They operate in the belief that one computer is much like any other. This is untrue, and some systems are very different to others. Furthermore very different attitudes are needed to work with mainframes as opposed to mid-range or personal computer/network systems and these attitudes are not always easily transferable. There are material difference in assumptions as well as knowledge, attitudes and skills, i.e. competencies between qualified individuals for each different type of hardware/software platform.

4.5.2 Architecture risk 2 – Technology platforms

Inappropriate or inadequate hardware or software platforms are being used.

It is sometimes difficult to know if this risk is a material one, especially when new leading-edge hardware or software systems are being employed. The way to minimise this risk is not to utilise leading edge technology, but to wait for this type of technology to be used by others and thus settle-in. However there is another risk associated with waiting which is the risk of lost opportunity.

Looking at the risk from a conservative point of view, too many leading-edge innovations have become bleeding-edge disasters in the field of IS and thus only organisations who are able to cope with high levels of risk should take chances here.

Leading edge versus bleeding edge

It is often quite advantageous to be a leader in the application of new technology. The literature abounds with stories of the first movers advantage. However if one moves into a new technology too soon the potential advantage may be dissipated with unforeseen technological as well as organisational problems. Safely moving from bleeding-edge to leading-edge can be like crossing a chasm.

4.5.3   Architecture risk 3 – Technology life cycles

The technology is about to be leap-frogged and made redundant or obsolete.

Investing in a technology at the end of its life cycle may produce a number of problems and should be assiduously avoided. However it is necessary to consider which of the many life cycles technology face is being discussed. Simply because there is a newer and more efficient technology on the market does not always warrant the abandonment of the old approach. The question is to do with matching the problem or opportunity to the appropriate technology. However there is usually the point that when a new technology is announced the cost or price of the older technology drops significantly. Clearly it is desirable not to buy into a technology at a high price when its market price is about to be substantially reduced.

4.6   Risk domains or perspectives

In Figure 4.1 the three risk categories are linked horizontally and the nature of these links are explained in Chapter 9. However the jigsaw metaphor also links the pieces of the jigsaw puzzle vertically.

The notions that constitute the vertical links are referred to as the risk domain or perspective. The risk domains or perspectives are conceptual themes or grouping through risks may be seen to share common characteristics.

The three risks domains or perspectives used in this model are knowledge, foundations and cycles. Thus in the first column of jigsaw pieces in Figure 4.1 the three vertical issues which are *understanding*, *ability to estimate* and *expertise*, are all to do with organisational knowledge. In the second column the three vertical issues, which are *buy-in*, *staff turnover* and *appropriate hardware and software platforms*, are all to do with a base from which to work, or business infrastructure. In the third column the three vertical issues, which are *business change*, *development tools and technology*, may all be seen in the context of *transition cycles*.

In a similar way to how the risk categories are linked horizontally, these risk domains or perspectives are also linked and this is further discussed in Chapter 9.

4.7 Summary

IS development projects face many potential problems. It is useful to categorise these problems in terms of business risks, development risks and architecture risks. Business risks are the most threatening as they go directly to the heart of the IS project. Figure 4.5 shows the completed major risks jigsaw.

Development risks are next most serious as they are to a large extent, although not entirely, a function of the internal management of the IS function, and as such can readily develop in a relatively slow and unseen way, from within the organisation. The architecture risks are the third in this taxonomy. Although serious, these risks are in a sense more easily controlled and they can sometimes be more easily anticipated than the other two risk categories.

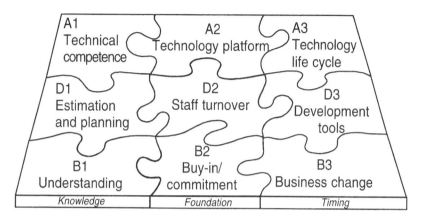

Figure 4.5 Key risks jigsaw

Key learning points in this chapter

❑ Although there are many different risks, it is useful to start an IS risk management process by identifying generic or high-level risk categories.

❑ IS development projects face at least three different types of risk which are business risks, development risks and architecture risks.

❑ Business risks are potentially the most damaging because if the information system does not solve a business problem or help take advantage of a business opportunity, the information system is likely to be rejected.

❑ Development risks are unlikely to cause the IS project to totally fail, but they can be very disruptive and cause substantial delays and large cost over-runs.

❑ Technology risks, when they materialise can be very problematical, but again, in general they are unlikely to cause the IS project to totally fail.

Practical action guidelines

Create a large version of the major risk jigsaw as shown here.

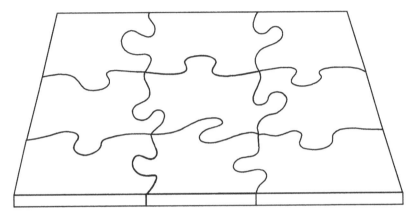

Through discussion with colleagues identify the three most important business risks you believe your IS project has to face. Write these risks into the bottom row of your jigsaw diagram.

At this stage do not go into too much detail. You will be shown how to deal with the finer points in Chapter 8.

Identify the three most important Development risks you believe your IS project has to face. Write these risks into the middle row of your jigsaw diagram.

Identify the three most important architectural risks you believe your IS project has to face. Write these risks into the top row of your jigsaw diagram.

You will now have made progress in identifying the major risks your project faces. In later chapters you will learn how to reduce the risk level associated with each one of these.

5 | The major consequences

The devil is in the consequences of our decisions, and not in the decisions themselves.

(Bernstein, 1996)

After disappointing delays and hefty overruns, the foolish system barely does what it's supposed to, and by the time it's fully operational it's already laughably obsolete.

(Wiersema, 1996)

5.1 Introduction

This chapter considers the consequences of the business risks, development risks and architecture risks, if they actually occur. The same jigsaw metaphor is used to match the risks with their individual consequences. As in the previous case nine major issues are discussed and these can be seen in Figure 5.1.

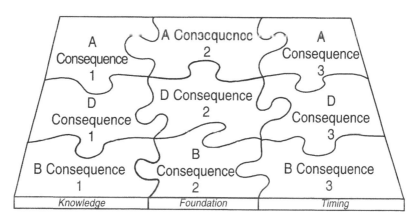

Figure 5.1 The major consequences of each risk

When any risk materialises there will be significant business consequences for the project and for the organisation. However the same taxonomy as used in the previous chapter is used here and thus the consequences are also discussed under the three areas of:

- consequences of business risks;
- consequences of development risks;
- consequences of architecture risks.

5.2   Business consequences

Three business consequences are identified that relate to the three business risks described in Chapter 4 and these are illustrated in Figure 5.2.

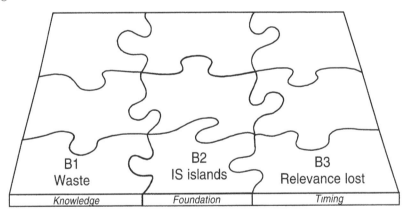

Figure 5.2 Key consequences of business risks

5.2.1   Business consequence 1 – Mismatch and waste

The first business risk identified in Chapter 4 was that the main stakeholders have an incomplete and inadequate understanding of the main business problem or opportunity.

The main consequence or result of this is that there will be a significant mismatch of resources and opportunities, resulting in the inappropriate use of funds etc., i.e. waste. This can lead to projects being undertaken with little or no business value. Sometime these projects are abandoned during their production but often they are completed and then the users simply refuse to accept the system. This type of situation results in a lack of understanding and trust between IS and other business professionals which has been referred to as the 'culture gap' by Grindley (1992). Grindley's research claims that the culture gap is one of the greatest problems faced by IS directors.

The notion of risk

Until the risk actually materialises it is always only a notion of potential problems or difficulties. The trouble begins once the risk has been converted into a reality. Then the consequences have to be faced. Risk management hopefully will minimise the work of the fire brigade.

5.2.2   Business consequence 2 – IS islands

If the second business risk occurs, which is that the user's enthusiasm fades, the consequence is that developers find it increasingly difficult to obtain co-operation from the users. This prevents co-ordination which at best leads to isolated islands of information systems which are only contributing a fraction of what they might otherwise achieve. When this risk occurs, users refuse to attend meetings or if they do turn up, they show little enthusiasm for the IS project. This can occur because users have changed their minds about their requirements and seek to employ other systems or even an outsourcer. As a result, users frequently quibble about how well the system meets their needs as well as fight about transfer costs, etc. Research suggests that this fading of enthusiasm does easily occur and needs a formative evaluation type of approach to ensure that stakeholders' commitment is maintained (Remenyi et al, 1997).

5.2.3   Business consequence 3 – Loss of fit or relevance

The third business risk refers to changes that occur to the requirements during development, not being accepted or not being accommodated in the system.

The consequence of this risk materialising is that the information system that is delivered is not actually required. The functionality is no longer appropriate to solve the current problem or take advantage of the current business opportunity. As a result the system is not used or it is soon abandoned. The system may also appear to have bugs and other operational problems. This is a very frequently encountered situation and requires specific management if it is to be avoided (Remenyi et al, 1997).

5.3 Development consequences

Three consequences of development problems are identified to match the three business risks previously discussed and are illustrated in Figure 5.3.

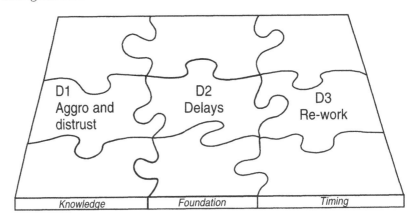

Figure 5.3 Key consequences of development risks

5.3.1 Development consequence 1 – Aggro and distrust

Unrealistic estimates of work required to develop an IS can lead to a number of difficult problems. The first and most obvious consequence is budget and time over-runs. This can even lead to the IS project appearing to become so costly that it is abandoned. Unrealistic estimates are frequently blamed for a vicious cycle of distrust between IS and other business professionals. However it should be mentioned that unrealistically low estimations of cost and time required have been used in the past, and are probably still used, to obtain management approval in situations where the IS budget is very strictly controlled. Obtaining approval for a project on an unrealistically low budget and subsequently obtaining extra funds has been euphemistically referred to as the creeping commitment approach to IS development funding.

5.3.2 Development consequence 2 – Learning curve and delays

An increasingly difficult problem to manage, is when the implementers do not remain in post and or key users move positions. The consequences of this can be long delays due to staff relearning hardware or software systems as well as organisational procedures and standards. This results in costs soaring and confusion, leading to poor performance, or bugs, or even in extreme cases the non-delivery of the information system.

5.3.3 Development consequence 3 - Rework

If the development tools are inappropriate or inadequate there may be some very unfortunate consequences. In the first place, it can lead to the need to redesign the system and rework the code that has been produced. This has led to IS projects being abandoned due to soaring costs. However, sometimes inappropriate or inadequate development tools do not show their presence until it has become necessary to enhance the system, and then it transpires that it is impossible or just too expensive to enhance or migrate the system.

5.4 Architecture consequences

Three consequences of architecture problems are identified to match the three architecture risks previously discussed and are illustrated in Figure 5.4.

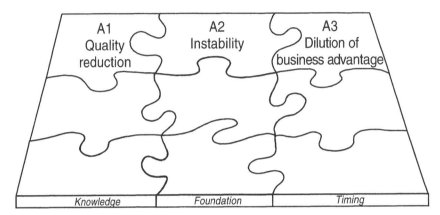

Figure 5.4 Key consequences of architecture risks

5.4.1 Architecture consequence 1 - Quality reduction

When an organisation does not have the appropriate expertise to successfully implement the chosen technology, the consequence is often the non-completion of the IS project or a hopelessly inadequate system, full of bugs and other problems.

5.4.2 Architecture consequence 2 - Instability

By far the most important architecture difficulty that an organisation could face is the situation when the technology is new to the organisation either because it is new to the industry as a whole or has not been used by the organisation before. Of course, the organisation can skill up to meet the new challenge, but this can take time and money, which can lead to projects either not being completed or being inadequately developed.

5.4.3 Architecture consequence 3 – Dilution of business advantage

If the technology used in the IS is leap-frogged and made obsolete, the consequences are usually that the business advantage that the organisation hoped to obtain from the IS is diluted or perhaps even rendered non-existent. At best the organisation obtains only inadequate performance from the system which may possibly be upgraded as soon as it is apparent that there is newer and more appropriate technology. Of course, sometimes the consequence of being leap-frogged is that the organisation is stuck with the old technology for quite some time into the future due to financial restrictions.

5.5   The impact of the consequences

Having identified the impact of the consequences of the risks, the next step is to evaluate the seriousness of the damage that will occur if they materialise, as well as to make an assessment of the actual probability of their occurring. This process can be handled by the use of two short questionnaires or rating forms and the completion of an appropriate risk-positioning diagram.

These questionnaires or rating forms need to be completed by the IS risk management officer in collaboration with other stakeholders. The results of the completion of these documents will be used to produce the risk-positioning diagram, which is an important tool in the IS risk management process.

If there is a material amount of difference in opinion as to the ratings for the issues in these forms they can be completed several times and average scores used in the risk-positioning diagram. In this case standard deviations or other measures of the range of the different opinions could also be calculated.

5.1.1   The seriousness of the consequences or damage questionnaire

Figure 5.5 shows the nine consequences discussed above with a 10-point scale showing the degree of damage to the project which would be encountered if the underlying risk was to materialise and the consequence was to occur.

5.1.2   The probability of the consequences or damage questionnaire

Figure 5.6 shows the same nine consequences discussed above with a 10-point scale, but this time showing the probability of the risk materialising and the consequence occurring.

Consequence issues seriousness	Date:			Project Reference:						
Rate the *seriousness* of each consequence where 1 is not serious and 10 is very serious										
	1	2	3	4	5	6	7	8	9	10
Mismatch and waste (*mw*) [1]										
IS islands (*ii*)										
Loss of fit or relevance (*lf*)										
Aggro and distrust (*ad*)										
Learning curve & delays (*lc*)										
Rework (*rw*)										
Quality reduction (*qr*)										
Instability (*is*)										
Dilution of business advantages (*db*)										

Figure 5.5 The seriousness of the damage assessment rating form

Consequence issues probability	Date:			Project Reference:						
Rate the *probability* of each consequence occurring where 1 is unlikely and 10 is very probable										
	1	2	3	4	5	6	7	8	9	10
Mismatch and waste (*mw*)										
IS islands (*ii*)										
Loss of fit or relevance (*lf*)										
Aggro and distrust (*ad*)										
Learning curve & delays (*lc*)										
Rework (*rw*)										
Quality reduction (*qr*)										
Instability (*is*)										
Dilution of business advantages (*db*)										

Figure 5.6 The probability of the consequences or damage assessment rating form

5.1.3 The risk-positioning diagram

Figure 5.7 shows the risk-positioning diagram. The vertical axis is the seriousness scale, while the horizontal axis is the probability scale.

---

[1] The two letter abbreviations are used in the risk-positioning diagram that follows.

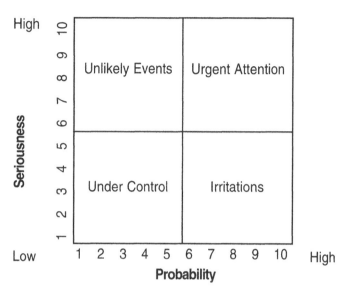

Figure 5.7 The risk positioning diagram

The top right quadrant represents risks that should be considered to require *urgent attention,* as they are both high on the seriousness scale and the probability scales. The management action required is to reduce either the seriousness or the impact of the consequence of the risk materialising, or to reduce the probability of the risk occurring or both.

The bottom left quadrant represents risks that are *under control* and which perhaps do not require immediate attention, but rather periodic monitoring.

The top left quadrant represents risks that require action in order to reduce the seriousness of their consequences. However as the probability of the risk in this quadrant occurring is low the action required is not as urgent as it would be in the top right quadrant. This quadrant is referred to as the *unlikely events* quadrant.

Finally, the bottom right quadrant, referred to as the *irritation* quadrant, represents risks that require action in order to reduce the probability of their occurrence. The risks or their consequences in this quadrant are not serious, but they are an irritation.

5.5 The impact of the consequences

The following is a worked example of the use of the rating forms and risk-positioning diagram. Figures 5.8 and 5.9 are the completed seriousness of the consequences or damage and the probability of the consequences or damage questionnaires respectively.

Consequence issues seriousness	Date:		Project Reference:							
Rate the *seriousness* of each consequence where 1 is not serious and 10 is very serious										
	1	2	3	4	5	6	7	8	9	10
Mismatch and waste (*mw*)							X			
IS islands (*ii*)					X					
Loss of fit or relevance (*lf*)								X		
Aggro and distrust (*ad*)						X				
Learning curve & delays (*lc*)								X		
Rework (*rw*)				X						
Quality reduction (*qr*)						X				
Instability (*is*)					X					
Dilution of business advantages (*db*)									X	

Figure 5.8 A completed seriousness of the damage assessment rating form

Consequence issues probability	Date:		Project Reference:							
Rate the *probability* of each consequence occurring where 1 is unlikely and 10 is very probable										
	1	2	3	4	5	6	7	8	9	10
Mismatch and waste (*mw*)		X								
IS islands (*ii*)				X						
Loss of fit or relevance (*lf*)				X						
Aggro and distrust (*ad*)			X							
Learning curve & delays (*lc*)							X			
Rework (*rw*)								X		
Quality reduction (*qr*)						X				
Instability (*is*)					X					
Dilution of business advantages (*db*)				X						

Figure 5.9 A completed probability of the consequences or damage assessment rating form

The scores given to each issue is used as a Cartesian point to locate its position on the risk positioning diagram as shown in Figure 5.10.

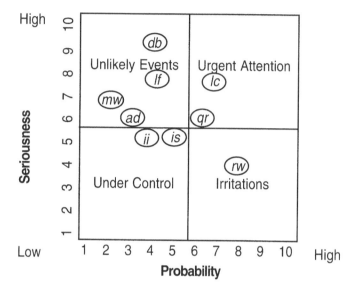

Figure 5.10 A completed risk-positioning diagram

The above figure suggest that lc (learning curve and delays) and qr (quality reduction) are the most serious consequences to the project if these risks materialise. Therefore these two issues need to receive immediate and urgent attention. With regards the unlikely event quadrant, the IT project risk manager will need to spend some time and effort in attempting to reduce the serious of the impact of db (dilution of business advantage), lf (loss of fit or relevant), mw (mismatch and waste) and ad (aggro and distrust) so that they more towards the under control quadrant.

5.5 Summary

The occurrence of each risk will result in a problem or series of problems. Sometimes these problems may not be so important, but on occasions any one of them could be devastating to the IS development project. In this chapter the main consequences of the risks materialising have been discussed and the full consequences jigsaw can be seen in Figure 5.5. Furthermore a seriousness and probability questionnaire has been provided and the chapter demonstrates how to use these instruments in order to produce a risk-positioning diagram.

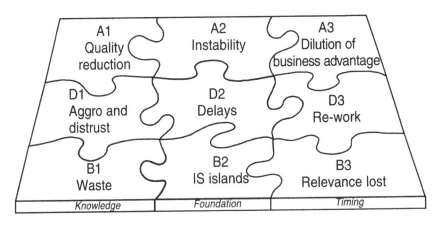

Figure 5.5 Full consequences jigsaw

Key learning points in this chapter

- If the business risks materialise then the consequences for the IS project and the organisation as a whole can be quite severe. Therefore it is very important to ensure that IS risk management is implemented in order to minimise these risks.

- Business risks usually have the most serious consequences to the project as well as the IS department and the organisation as a whole.

- However, the consequences of development risks when they occur are very disruptive. They can cause major delays as well as substantial budget over runs.

❑ In a similar way, architecture risk can also produce distinctly adverse consequences. Thus IS risk management is essential to minimise the probability of any of these risks occurring.

❑ The seriousness and probability assessment questionnaires or rating forms are useful tools in assessing the impact of the consequences of a risk should it materialise. These tools can be used in order to create a risk-positioning diagram, which is valuable when prioritising a risk management programme.

Practical action guidelines

Create a large version of the major risk jigsaw as shown here.

Through discussion with colleagues identify the three most important consequences you believe your IS project has to face if the business risks which you have listed at the end of the previous chapter come to pass.

Repeat this exercise for development risks and architecture risks.

Once the consequence jigsaw has been complete you will have a comprehensive overview of what will happen if any of the identified risks actually materialise.

Use the seriousness and probability questionnaires to collect the information required to produce a risk positioning diagram, which in turn can be used to help direct a risk management programme.

6 | Financial analysis of risk

We are merely reminding ourselves that human decision affecting the future, whether personal or political or economic, cannot depend on strict mathematical expectations, since the basis for making such calculations does not exist; and that it is our innate urge to activity which makes the wheels go round, our rational selves choosing between the alternatives as best we are able, calculating where we can, but often falling back for our motive or whim or sentiment or chance.

(Keynes, 1964)

There are three kinds of lies: lies, damned lies and statistics.

(Disraeli, quoted in Neider, 1959)

6.1 Introduction

Whatever approach is taken to IS risk management it is useful to consider how the occurrence of the risks might actually affect the financial estimations that are produced as part of the feasibility study. What this means in effect is that the potential problems or risks an IS project could face are brought into the initial costing exercise at the very beginning of the evaluation of the investment proposal.

To introduce these risk elements it is necessary to extend the usual financial planning approach based on the traditional deterministic analysis used in business accounting and budgeting and use stochastic or risk or probability analysis in the financial planning exercise.

6.2 Traditional financial analysis

IS project evaluation can be undertaken in several different ways using a variety of measures or investment statistics and at least two fundamentally different assessment processes. The two processes discussed here are the *deterministic* approach using single point estimates for the input values and generating a single estimate for the result, and the *stochastic* approach which uses ranges as input and generates a range of results. The stochastic method is sometimes referred to as *simulation* or *risk analysis.*

The traditional method of financial planning and budgeting uses the deterministic approach in which organisations use a single forecast as their expected sales. From this number they deduce their costs and their other expenses to arrive at a single number for their predicted or forecasted profit. Although management is aware that the single forecast as their expected sales and cost are not likely to be perfectly accurate they accept these numbers as being close enough for the purposes of financial planning.

Traditional financial analysis of projects is undertaken using discounted cash flow techniques involving estimates of the investment amount, the annual benefits and the cost of capital. All these variables are difficult to estimate. The cost of the firm's capital is frequently considered the most difficult variable to determine and thus the rate of interest which the firm pays on its debt or an arbitrarily chosen hurdle or discount rate is sometimes used as a surrogate for the cost of capital.

6.3 Deterministic analysis

Deterministic analysis assumes a certain, or stable world where the exact value of input variables, such as sales and costs and expenses, can be known. Once the values of these inputs are entered, a unique result, determined by the logic of the algorithm and the precise data, is calculated. This applies to simple operating budgets as well as more sophisticated financial plans and capital budgeting calculations. Increasing this approach is being seen as limiting, especially for the purposes of capital budgeting for projects such as IS development.

Risk analysis tools

Despite the fact that financial risk analysis tools have been available for about 30 years, very few organisations actually use these methods. Initially financial risk analysis tools were very expensive and cumbersome to use. However this is not true today. It is thought that the reason for this lack is to do with the management need to believe in a world more deterministic than it actually is.

When producing financial figures for an IS project, an analyst has to estimate the investment costs, the on-going costs and place some financial value on the potential benefits. All these variables are quite difficult to estimate in advance of the project and thus there is a high degree of risk associated with these figures. In fact because ex-ante investment analysis[1] exclusively uses estimates of future values for the investment amount, the on-going costs and the benefits, it is frequently said that as soon as the single point values are determined, the estimates of the input and output variables will be wrong[2] (Remenyi et al, 1996). Nonetheless it is argued that these single point values will be close enough to be useful in the analysis of the IS projects. An example of such a deterministic financial plan for an IS project is shown in Figure 6.1.

Stochastic, or risk analysis, on the other hand, attempts to accommodate the inherent risk or variability in the input estimates and produces a result that more closely reflects the level of uncertainty frequently experienced in the real world.

Where uncertainty is small,[3] deterministic models can provide suitable solutions. However, it is more likely that uncertainty in the input variables, evidenced by their variability, will be relatively high and therefore this uncertainty must be taken into consideration.

---

[1] Ex-ante investment analysis refers to analysis before the investment begins.

[2] The word 'wrong' is used here in the sense of not being perfectly accurate.

[3] As uncertainty in all the input variables as well as the outcome of the proposed system is often quite high, risk analysis is increasingly being regarded as very appropriate to IS investment developments. Despite this it is not yet in general use.

6.3 Deterministic analysis

A low level or micro model	£'000s	£'000s
Initial investment costs		1350
Hardware	500	
Software	450	
Data communications	150	
Commissioning	250	
On-going costs		130
Staff	50	
Maintenance	45	
Accommodation	25	
General expenses	10	
Benefits		275
Reduction in administrative costs	20	
Better utilisation of inventory	75	
Better utilisation of transport	30	
Additional income arising from sales improvement	150	
Net benefit (monthly)		145
Annualised benefit		1740
ROI		129%

Figure 6.1 A deterministic financial plan for an IS development project for one year

Specifying a probability distribution for each of the input variables such as investment, cash flows, and cost of capital captures this uncertainty. There are many candidate probability distributions that can be usefully employed for this purpose. Some of the more useful distributions are likely to be the uniform, the triangular and the beta.

Operationalisation of the above is through use of the Monte Carlo method. This involves generating a range of outcomes for the input variables, e.g. investment, described by some specified probability distribution, and then evaluating the behaviour of an associated output variable, e.g. internal rate of return. The Monte Carlo method can also be used to establish how robust and sensitive the outcomes are with respect to the assumptions concerning the input variable(s).

For more on the properties of a number of probability distributions, and guidance on how to generate random samples from these distributions, see Johnson and Kotz (1970) and Gonin and Money (1989). However relatively straightforward rectangular probability distributions[4] where all outcomes have an equal probability are easy to use and provide quite a lot of useful information.

6.4 Risk analysis

The risk of an investment is the potential of input/output variables to fluctuate from their original estimates. In the vast majority of cases input/output variables do fluctuate, and risk analysis accommodates this by allowing ranges, rather than single-point estimates, to be used. It is generally much easier to confidently state that an investment will be between 200,000 and 300,000 than it will be 250,000.

There are a variety of techniques available to assist management and other risk assessors in evaluating the extent and the size of the risk inherent in a particular investment. There are at least three generic approaches to identifying and assessing risk. These are:

- Group brainstorming.
- Expert judgement.
- Assumption analysis.

Group brainstorming uses group interaction to identify the variables that carry the most exposure to variability. Once the variables have been identified, the group then attempts to quantify the limits of the variability as well as the probability associated with the range of possible inputs and outputs. Brainstorming groups may meet several times before the estimates of the variables are finalised.

Expert judgement uses experienced individuals who are aware of the factors causing the investment potential to vary. This is the quickest and easiest way of identifying risk, but considerable care must be given to choosing the expert.

---

[4] This type of distribution is sometimes referred to as a uniform distribution.

Assumption analysis requires the detailed questioning of each assumption, by modifying each one in such a way that circumstances will be evaluated which are disadvantageous to the investment. The effects of the changes in assumptions are then used as part of the range of variable specification.

A useful tool in assessing different types of risk is the influence diagram. This is a perceptual map showing concepts or issues to illustrate how different aspects of a proposed investment may interact with each other, causing variability in the input/output estimates.

6.4.1 Influence diagrams

An influence diagram allows all the related concepts and issues to be mapped showing the interconnections between them. Such conceptual mapping may be used to quickly identify areas of high variability, which are those with a high number of interconnections. This technique is especially useful for facilitating creative thinking in the search for the identification and quantification of risk. Figure 6.2 shows an influence diagram illustrating the nine factors that directly or indirectly affect sales volumes.

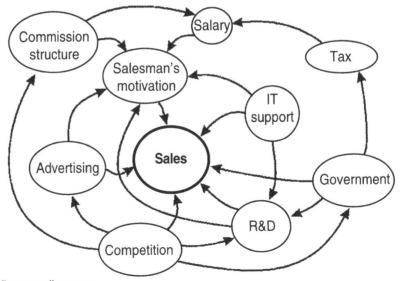

Figure 6.2 An influence diagram

However, after the conceptual map has been developed it is then necessary to debate the size of the potential fluctuations in the variables. This can be achieved by bringing together a group of experienced managers and discussing the likely value of each factor. At the conclusion of such a debate, maximum and minimum values should be established for sales, costs, prices, assets, cash flows, etc.

6.5 Using spreadsheets for risk analysis

The spreadsheet is a useful tool for performing financial risk analysis for IS development projects. Figure 6.3 shows the results of a Capital Investment Appraisal model.

	A	B	C	D	E	F	G
1	Capital Investment Appraisal System						
2	A deterministic model						
3			Cash-Out	Cash-In	Net Cash Movement each year		
4	IT Investment - Cash Out		350,000		-350000		
5	Net IT Benefits	Year 1		66106	66106		
6		Year 2		99902	99902		
7		Year 3		120901	120901		
8		Year 4		194590	194590		
9		Year 5		249671	249671		
10	Fixed Cost of Capital or Interest Rate		25%				
11							
12			Y1	Y2	Y3	Y4	Y5
13	Forecast inflation rates		22.00%	30.00%	37.00%	40.00%	42.00%
14							
15	Investment Reports on IT System						
16	Payback in years & months			3 years		4 months	
17	Rate of return(%)		41.78%				
18	N P V Fixed Discount Rate (FDR)		-9760				
19	Profitability Index FDR (PI)		0.97				
20	Internal Rate of Return (IRR)		73.91%				
21	Variable Discount Rates						
22	N P V Variable Discount Rates (VDR)		-55414				
23	Profitability Index VDR (PI)		0.84				
24	Discounted Payback FDR in years and months			5 years		1 months	

Figure 6.3 A Capital Investment Appraisal spreadsheet model

The model in Figure 6.3 has been developed using deterministic logic. This means that single-point estimates have been made for all the input values from which the output is calculated.

Risk management, by its very nature, suggests that the single-point estimate approach normally used in evaluating information system investments is not adequate. The single-point estimate, or deterministic approach, assumes that all cost and benefit estimates are known with certainty. Clearly this is seldom ever the case in reality. When risk management is being applied, this lack of accuracy is admitted and cost estimates and revenue estimates are expressed, not as single points but as ranges of values (Nugus, 1997).

Figure 6.4 considers an investment for which the actual amount to be invested, the benefits to be derived and the interest rates are not precisely known. However it is known that the investment amount will be between £350,000 and £400,000. Similarly the IT benefits for years 1 to 5 have also been entered into the spreadsheet as ranges, for example in year 1 the minimum benefit is estimated at £65,000 and the maximum value of the benefit is stated at £75,000. Similarly, the exact rate of interest is not known, but it is estimated at between 20% and 30% per annum.

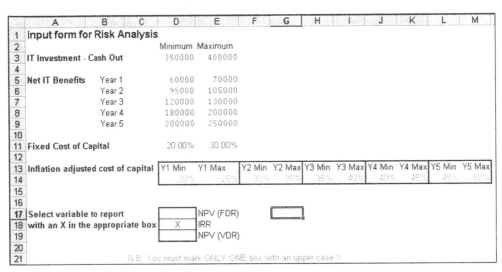

Figure 6.4 Risk analysis input form

By recalculating the spreadsheet thousands or even tens of thousands of times using values between the specified maximum and minimum, different outcomes will be obtained. Due to the uncertainty of exactly what the actual costs and benefits will be it is important to recalculate the model a large number of times. By so doing, a large number of different combinations of costs and benefits are selected. It is then by analysing the distribution of the outcomes that an understanding of the probable results of the investment can be seen (Nugus, 1997). Figure 6.5 shows a results scenario for the Internal Rate of Return (IRR), using the input data in Figure 6.4.

Summary statistics for	IRR
Mean	0.204
Standard deviation	0.016
Range	0.079
Minimum	0.164
Maximum	0.243
No. of recalculations	2000

Figure 6.5 Summary results for risk analysis on IRR

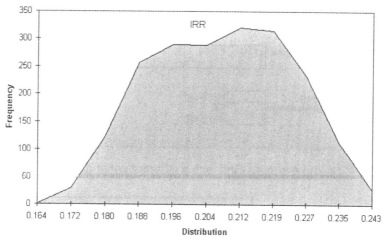

Figure 6.6 Graphical representation of risk analysis results for IRR

The data used in Figure 6.4 to produce the results in Figures 6.5 and 6.6 would be regarded as being of relatively low risk.[5] The reason for this is that the most likely outcome is a return of 20% with a standard deviation of 1.6%. This means that even if all the

---

[5] This view of risk is of course contingent upon the rate being at least as big as the organisation's standard hurdle rate.

most unfavourable estimates occur, i.e. maximum investment costs, lowest benefits and highest cost of capital, this investment will still be expected to produce an IRR of 16%. On the positive side, if the investment is kept low and the highest benefits are achieved etc., then this investment could produce a return as high as 24%.

A different set of input data can of course produce quite a different scenario. Figure 6.7 shows a different set of data and Figures 6.8 and 6.9 show the result of the risk analysis using the Net Present Value (NPV) as the outcome variable.

	A	B	C	D	E	F	G	H	I	J	K	L	M
1	Input form for Risk Analysis												
2				Minimum	Maximum								
3	IT Investment - Cash Out			450000	600000								
4													
5	Net IT Benefits	Year 1		60000	80000								
6		Year 2		85000	115000								
7		Year 3		120000	140000								
8		Year 4		170000	210000								
9		Year 5		200000	260000								
10													
11	Fixed Cost of Capital			15.00%	40.00%								
12													
13	Inflation adjusted cost of capital			Y1 Min	Y1 Max		Y2 Min	Y2 Max	Y3 Min	Y3 Max	Y4 Min	Y4 Max	Y5 Min Y5 Max
14				20%	25%		30%	35%	35%	40%	40%	45%	45% 50%
15													
16													
17	Select variable to report			X	NPV (FDR)								
18	with an X in the appropriate box				IRR								
19					NPV (VDR)								
20													
21				N.B. You must mark ONLY ONE box with an upper case X									

Figure 6.7 Risk analysis input form with a different set of data

Summary statistics for	NPV
Mean	−199191.810
Standard deviation	73689.890
Range	374190.122
Minimum	−359681.589
Maximum	14508.533
No. of recalculations	2000

Figure 6.8 Results table for risk analysis on NPV

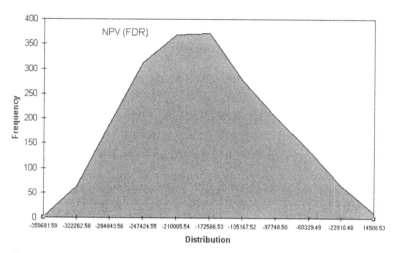

Figure 6.9 Graphical representation of risk analysis results on NPV

The example used to produce the results shown in Figures 6.8 and 6.9 would be regarded as a relatively high risk. The most likely outcome of this investment is an NPV of – 199,191, which of course is unsatisfactory and would suggest that it is inappropriate to proceed with the investment under these terms. In fact the worst scenario is an NPV of –359,681. However, it is possible, with a favourable discount rate and good annual net benefits, for this investment to return a positive NPV of 14,508. This variability is the risk.

6.6 Worked examples

The following is a worked example financial risk analysis in the IS risk management process. It describes an organisation where there is a considerable degree of uncertainty about both the costs and the benefits that will be derived from the IS investment.

Continental Products Limited were considering the acquisition of a new information system. After considerable discussion the IS staff produced the following cost estimates for hardware, software and commissioning.

1 The hardware cost will be between £400K and £900K.

2   The software costs are estimated at between £350K and £500K.

3   The commissioning costs will be between £200K and £300K.

It was thought that there was an equal probability that the actual costs would be anywhere between the highest and lowest estimates. Thus the probability distribution is said to be uniform or rectangular. A similar set of assumptions was employed to establish the ongoing costs and the benefits to be derived from the information system.

Capital investment appraisal for Continental Products Ltd				
Costs in 000s	Lowest	Highest	Average-M L	Risk data
Hardware	400	900	650	509
Software	350	500	425	476
Commissioning	200	300	250	272
Total	950	1700	1325	1051

Figure 6.10 Various cost estimates using the deterministic and stochastic measures.

The four columns in Figure 6.10 reflect the possible values for the three cost variables. The *Lowest* and the *Highest* columns are self explanatory. The *Average-ML* (where ML is the *Most Likely*) column is the mid-point between the Lowest and Highest values. The *Risk Data* column is calculated by using the RAND() function from the spreadsheet to generate a random number between the lowest and highest values.

The essence of numbers

Numbers or estimates are always only representatives of what is hoped will become real action. Estimates are always about further activity and are thus very difficult to be accurate about. Unfortunately we sometime attribute to numbers a greater creditability than they deserve. This phenomenon is well explained by Bernstein (1996) who said:

"Our lives teem with numbers, but we sometimes forget that numbers are only tools. They have no soul; they may indeed become fetishes. Many of our most critical decisions are made by computers, contraptions that devour numbers like voracious monsters and insist on being nourished with ever-greater quantities of digits to crunch, digest, and spew back."

The operations director at Continental was especially concerned about how long it would take for the benefits to appear. It was at his insistence the stakeholders agreed that there would be no benefits in the first year and that there might not be any benefits even in the second year.

The stakeholders debated the benefits issue for several days before finally agreeing to the following estimates of benefits:

1   In the first year after implementation the firm believe that there is little likelihood of the benefit exceeding the ongoing costs. Thus, the net benefit is estimated at zero.

2   For the second year the system is expected to produce up to £100K of benefits, although there are some members of staff who believe that the system will only produce net positive benefits in the third year.

3   In year 3 the benefits will be between £450K and £650K and in year four they will be between £850K and £100K.

4   In year 5 the benefits are expected to be fixed at £1500K for some years to come.

5   The firm's cost of capital is at present 25% and it is believed that over the next five years it will fluctuate between 20% and 30%.

6   The stakeholders were not able to agree on the economic life of the project. Everyone agreed that the computer system would still be working in five years' time, but certain members believed that an IT investment should be fully amortised in no more than three years. Other members of the stakeholders suggested that a seven-year approach should be taken as there was very little likelihood of any real benefits in the first or second year.

7   The stakeholders agreed that the net present value (NPV) should be the primary measure by which the investment will be judged. However, they all unanimously wanted to know what the internal rate of return (IRR) and also the discounted payback, would be.

6.6 Worked examples

Capital investment appraisal for Continental Products Ltd				
Benefits in 000s	Lowest	Highest	Average-M L	Risk data
Year 1	0	0	0	0
Year 2	100	100	100	100
Year 3	450	650	550	559
Year 4	850	1100	975	913
Year 5	1500	1500	1500	1500

Figure 6.11 Benefit estimates over 5 years using the deterministic and stochastic measures

Figure 6.11 has been created in a similar way to Figure 6.10, but reflects the various possible values for the benefits over the five years. The *Lowest* and the *Highest* columns are again self-explanatory. The *Most Likely* or average column is the mid-point between the Lowest and Highest values. The *Risk Data* column is calculated by using the RAND() function from the spreadsheet and generates a random number between the Lowest and Highest values.

Capital investment appraisal for Continental Products Ltd				
Costs of capital	Lowest	Highest	Average-M L	Risk data
	20	30	25	22

Figure 6.12 Various estimates, in percentages, of the cost of capital using the deterministic and stochastic measures.

Figure 6.12, which represents the cost of capital, has been created in the same way as Figures 6.10 and 6.11.

Figure 6.13 represents a set of capital investment appraisal analysis where the NPV, the IRR and Payback are all calculated. These terms are fully explained in Appendix E.

The capital investment appraisal analysis as set out in Figure 6.13 shows three sets of calculations. The first set of calculations, described as Scenario 1, represents the possible outcome if the average or most likely numbers are achieved. In terms of the NPV these calculations show a result which does not earn an adequate return to justify

Capital investment appraisal for Continental Products Ltd						
Scenario 1			Y E A R S			
Cash flows	YR0	YR1	YR2	YR3	YR4	YR5
(Most Likely)	−1325	0	100	550	975	1500
Cum. cash flow	−1325	−1325	−1225	−675	300	1800
Year number	0	1	2	3	4	5
NPV	−£88.52					
IRR	23%					
Payback in year	4					
Scenario 2						
(Worst scenario)	−1700	0	100	450	850	1500
Cum. cash flow	−1700	−1700	−1600	−1150	−300	1200
Year number	0	1	2	3	4	5
NPV	−£4,259.72					
IRR	13%					
Payback is greater than five years						
Scenario 3						
(Best scenario)	−950	0	100	650	1100	1500
Cum. cash flow	−950	−950	−850	200	900	2400
Year number	0	1	2	3	4	5
NPV	£628.90					
IRR	36%					
Payback in year	4					
Scenario 4						
(Risk analysis)	−1076	0	100	643	1044	1500
Cum. cash flow	−1075.73	−1075.73	−975.73	−333.213	710.8376	2210.838
Year number	0	1	2	3	4	5
NPV	£386.16					
IRR	31%					
Payback in year	4					

Figure 6.13 Various estimates of the performance of the investment using most likely, best and worst projections as well as risk analysis

proceeding with the investment. One way of interpreting this is that the cost of capital the organisation needs to earn is higher than the IRR that it appears the investment can generate.

The second set of calculations, described as Scenario 2, represents the possible outcome if the worst numbers are achieved, i.e. the highest cost and the lowest benefits and the highest cost of capital. In terms of the NPV these calculations show a very poor result which clearly does not earn an adequate return to justify proceeding with the investment.

The third set of calculations described as Scenario 3, represents the possible outcome if the best numbers are achieved, i.e. the lowest cost and the highest benefits and the lowest cost of capital. In terms of the NPV these calculations show a good result, which does earn an adequate return to justify proceeding with the investment.

The fourth set of calculations described as Scenario 4, represents the possible outcome using randomly generated numbers between the limits suggested. In terms of the NPV these calculations show a good result, which does earn an adequate return to justify proceeding with the investment.

If the data supplied in the above example is used to perform a simulation using 2000 reiterations, and the results are used to produce a graphical representation of all the possible outcomes, then the following bell-shaped type curve will be produced as per Figure 6.14.

The result of this analysis is likely to be regarded as unsatisfactory as too much of the graph represents a negative NPV.

From Figure 6.15, which indicates the result of the simulation in statistical terms, it can also be seen that the proposed IS project is likely to be unsatisfactory.

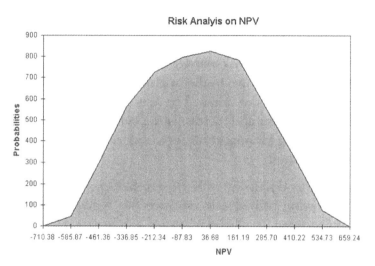

Figure 6.14 The graphical results of the risk simulation

Descriptive statistics	
Mean	−85
Standard error	4
Median	−82
Mode	#N/A
Standard deviation	249
Sample variance	62223
Kurtosis	−1
Skownɔɔɔ	0
Range	1243
Minimum	−687
Maximum	556
Sum	−386379
Count	5000
Confidence level (95.000%)	7

Figure 6.15 The statistical results of the risk simulation

6.7   Re-examining the input assumptions

At this stage, from a risk management perspective the task of the IS risk officer is to return to the original estimates and to attempt to question each of the values. The aim is to see if there is a way of reducing the costs and increasing the benefits in absolute terms, as well as looking for opportunities to reduce the potential variability in the estimates.

After further discussion with the stakeholders the IS staff produced the following revised cost estimates for hardware, software and commissioning. It is believed that it will be possible to reduce the investment cost without materially effecting the benefit stream which is being left with the original estimated numbers. Thus the following estimates are now relevant for the investment.

1   The hardware cost will now be between £250K and £500K.

2   The software costs are now estimated at between £150K and £250K.

3   The commissioning costs will be unchanged between £200K and £300K.

These new values are shown in Figure 6.16.

Capital investment appraisal for Continental Products Ltd				
Costs in 000s	Lowest	Highest	Average-M L	Risk data
Hardware	250	500	375	410
Software	150	250	200	166
Commissioning	200	300	250	233
Total	600	1050	825	891

Figure 6.16 The new range of estimates

With these assumptions a new set of capital investment appraisal analysis is performed where the NPV, the IRR and Payback are all again calculated. As may be seen from Figure 6.17, the IS investment opportunity now looks far more attractive.

Capital investment appraisal for Continental Products Ltd						
Scenario 1				Y E A R S		
Cash flows	YR0	YR1	YR2	YR3	YR4	YR5
(Most Likely)	−825	0	100	550	975	1500
Cum. cash flow	−825	−825	−725	−175	800	2300
Year number	0	1	2	3	4	5
NPV	£411.48					
IRR	38%					
Payback in year	4					
Scenario 2						
(Worst scenario)	−1050	0	100	450	850	1500
Cum. cash flow	−1050	−1050	−950	−500	350	1850
Year number	0	1	2	3	4	5
NPV	-£2,026.60					
IRR	27%					
Payback is greater than five years						
Scenario 3						
(Best scenario)	−600	0	100	650	1100	1500
Cum. cash flow	−600	−600	−500	150	1250	2750
Year number	0	1	2	3	4	5
NPV	£978.90					
IRR	53%					
Payback in year	3					
Scenario 4						
(Risk analysis)	−936	0	100	489	1049	1500
Cum. cash flow	−935.528	−935.528	−835.528	−346.742	701.8014	2201.801
Year number	0	1	2	3	4	5
NPV	£305.88					
IRR	34%					
Payback in year	4					

Figure 6.17 The new range of investment statistics

It is important to note that the estimates of cost and benefit should not be lightly changed. If the IS risk officer cannot find a reasonable cause for expecting to be able to reduce the cost, or increase the benefit, or reduce the variability in these estimates, then they should not be changed. Producing better figures for the sake of the financial analysis is simply a method of self-delusion.

Figure 6.17 shows a much better situation. All the three scenarios show improvement. However Scenario 2 which is the worst case scenario still shows a potential loss or negative NPV. Thus the IS project manager needs to pay careful attention to not operate near the parameters described by these circumstances.

In general if any of the three positive scenarios can be achieved then the project will have been worthwhile.

Figure 6.18 also shows a better projection for the IS investment as do the statistics displayed in Figure 6.19.

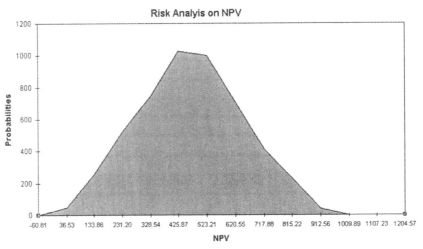

Figure 6.18 The graphical results of the risk simulation

It is important to note that not only are the estimates of the returns that will be achieved better in the second set of calculations, but these figures show a significant reduction in the risk profile faced by the IS development. This reduction in risk may be observed

Descriptive statistics	
Mean	417
Standard error	3
Median	417
Mode	#N/A
Standard deviation	180
Sample variance	32409
Kurtosis	−1
Skewness	0
Range	973
Minimum	−61
Maximum	913
Sum	−386379
Count	5000
Confidence level (95.000%)	7

Figure 6.19 The new statistical results of the risk simulation

visually by looking at the relative shapes of the curves in Figure 6.14 and 6.18. In this respect the rule is that the narrower the curve the lower the risk. In addition, the standard deviation, which is regarded as an important measure of risk, is 252 and 177 in the two cases. Thus the second set of projections shows lower risk.

6.8 Financial risk review process

The process of stating assumptions and examining their financial implications by using stochastic type analysis as described in this chapter is very important for the better understanding of the costs and the benefits associated with an IS investment. However it is important to remember the words of Berstein (1996) quoted above, as well as those of Wittgenstein (1980) who said, "Nothing is so difficult as not deceiving oneself".

The numbers are only as good as the intentions and actions they represent, and a project with a great business case can fail just as quickly as one without any cost benefit analysis at all.

6.9 Summary

When considering how the occurrence of the risks might actually affect the financial estimations that are produced as part of the feasibility study, this question is frequently asked:

Is the benefit to be derived from a formal financial IS risk evaluation or assessment worth the effort or are simple single point estimates good enough for the average project manager?

In the past it was difficult and expensive to perform sophisticated financial risk analysis, whereas today it is inexpensive and relatively easy. Furthermore, historically there was very little understanding of how to use the output from financial risk analysis. Today there is a much greater awareness of how to uses the result of this type of thinking.

Thus in some respects this question could now be considered to be obsolete or at least on the verge of obsolescence.

But on the other hand, there are many who would argue that information technology is so clearly a basic requirement for business that it is unnecessary to perform regular cost benefit analysis at all, never mind sophisticated financial risk analysis. Such an argument implies that an IS is as essential to the firm as an adequate telephone system.

Yet again, investment in IS developments still does not represent trivial amounts of money to most organisations and, therefore, should not be compared to telephones. In reality, unless some planning and estimating is done, management will never know how it is performing. And, therefore, even though the estimation and/or prediction of IS performance is imperfect, it is essential to perform these calculations to obtain some sort of indication of what might be expected. However, whatever method or metric is chosen it must be realised that it is likely to be no more than a subjective assessment with a low level of objectivity.

As a tool to support IS risk management the use of financial risk analysis is certainly a most useful device and it is simple enough that it should be used by all.

Key learning points in this chapter

- ❑ Single point estimates of investment cost, on-going costs and possible benefits are very unlikely to be accurate.

- ❑ A much more realistic way of presenting these financial estimates is to use ranges.

- ❑ Once ranges for these financial values are specified then it is possible to use risk analysis.

- ❑ Risk analysis provides a very much richer picture of the potential of the IS project as well as the financial impact of the possible risks or problems.

Practical action guidelines

Think of the estimates of the resources required for the IS project in terms of ranges of values rather than single point estimates.

To achieve this, obtain different opinions from colleagues about the resources required for the project. These different opinions will be the source of your ranges.

As a result of this when you are looking at the cost of the hardware don't write it down as £159,500. Rather state is as being between two values such as perhaps between £150,000 and £175,000.

Use a risk analysis approach to calculating the return on the IS investment. There are numerous tools on the market with which to do this. One of the inexpensive tolls which is also easy to use is called @RISK and is an add-in product for Excel and Lotus.

Discuss with the other members of the IS development team how you will be able to avoid the high cost and achieve the high benefits areas in the model.

7 | The major risk drivers

There are three drivers of change: People and their Aspirations, Technology and the Competition.

(Harvey-Jones, 1988)

Risk management in technical projects is a relatively new discipline, dating from around 1980...... Risk management for software projects has been formalised within the past two years.

(Fairley, 1990)

7.1 Introduction

In order to be able to develop and to action an IS risk management programme it is essential to understand the drivers of the risks which have been identified. It is only by understanding the drivers or causes of the risks that the potential problems may be avoided or neutralised. Each risk has potentially several drivers and each one of these drivers may cause the risks to materialise as a problem or difficulty. It is therefore important that the study of the drivers should be performed as thoroughly as possible, as an understanding of these is the key to developing a strategy to counteract the negative effects of the risks.

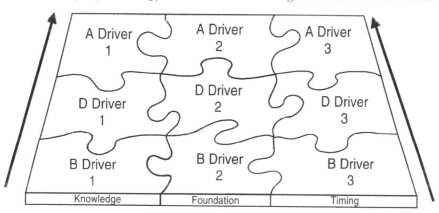

Figure 7.1 Risk driver jigsaw

7.2 Business risk drivers

Figure 7.2 shows three key drivers that underpin the three key or central business risks that have been identified in Chapter 4. It is a central part of IS risk management to identify and understand these risk drivers.

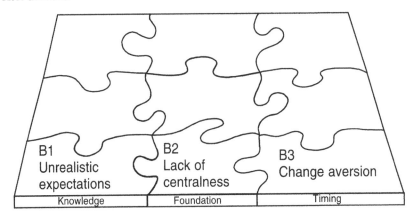

B1
Unrealistic expectations

B2
Lack of centralness

B3
Change aversion

Knowledge · Foundation · Timing

Figure 7.2 Key business drivers

7.2.1 Business drivers risk 1 – Unrealistic expectations

There are a considerable number of drivers that can cause the main stakeholders to have an incomplete and inadequate understanding of the main business problem or opportunity. These include a lack of interest in information systems, computerphobia, unreasonable pressure to start the system's development, the imposition of unrealistic deadlines and a general rush to catch-up mentally. Furthermore, this risk is obviously aggravated when IS people do not understand the business, and by business people who do not understand IS. These misunderstandings, which are sometimes referred to as the culture gap, have at their centre a generally poor attitude to interpersonal relationships and communications.

In situations where the IS people and the other members of staff are suspicious of each other, there is a high probability that problems of misunderstanding will occur and remedial action must be taken.

Figure 7.3 shows a path suggested by Butler Cox by which organisations with problems obtaining management commitment may proceed.

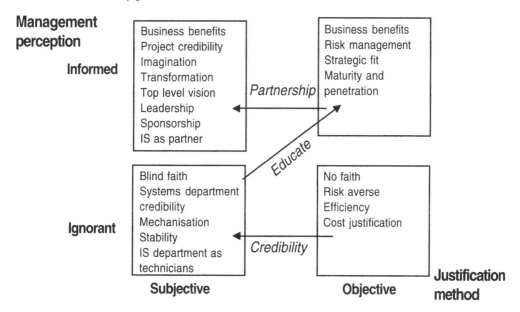

Figure 7.3 The path to informed management collaboration with the IS department

In Figure 7.3 uninformed objective management is seen as having little or no faith in the IS operation and therefore being risk averse and demanding efficiency improvements with clear and compelling and cost justification. As the IS operation performs well they establish their credibility and management tends to have more faith in them, even at time blind faith. At this stage if the IS operation expends the effort to educate management they can develop the IS operation in much more interesting areas and obtain greater benefits than simple efficiency related ones. Finally the last quadrant show how the situation may develop if management and the IS operation begin to behave as partners with a joint vision, etc.

7.2.2 Business drivers risk 2 - Lack of centralness

There are numerous reasons why, despite initial appearances, users do not properly buy-in the advantages of or the need for an information system. Perhaps the most important is that there is no business oriented IS vision or strategy or the IS strategy has not been adequately explained to all the principal users. Thus the users do not see IS as being central to their needs. Another reason is that the organisation has no IS vision other than that of cost reduction. Also the commitment of the main stakeholders is at some time subsequently diluted, due to other pressures or other responsibilities not to mention general business fatigue.

Beneath the risk

Understanding the risk requires the identification of the risk driver as this is the ultimate source of the potential problem. Trying to do something about the risk without addressing the drivers is like putting a plaster on a gangrenous wound and expecting it to heal by itself. It will not work. Thus it is very important to put aside the time necessary to explore the risk drivers issues thoroughly.

7.2.3 Business drivers risk 3 - Change aversion

When changes occur to the requirements during development and these are not accepted or are not accommodated then the IS project is likely to fail, sometimes quite dramatically. Changes are not accepted for many reasons, including inflexible budgets, immovable deadlines, or no appropriate understanding of the market/technology by the decision-makers.

Some autocratically managed organisations have a mind set in which change is simply not allowed. Of course, at the end of the 20th century, this attitude may be fatal to the organisation.

In reality, change in an IS requirement is sometimes, if not quite often, seen, not as a natural part of business growth and development, but rather as a sign of failure that the actual IS needs were not understood. This sometimes results in an attempt to suppress the proposed changes. The pejorative term *scope creep* is used to describe such unwanted changes and *scope creep* is almost universally regarded as a bad thing.

It is imperative to accommodate changes to any of the important variables that underpin the way information systems are or can be used in the business, including the environment, competition, staff, deregulation, etc.

The business risks drivers are often related to relationships between the IS staff and the rest of the organisation. The attitudes on which these relationships are based are often deep seated in the organisation and thus a considerable amount of effort will have to be expended to ensure that the organisation's exposure to risk is minimised.

7.3 Development drivers

Figure 7.4 shows three key development drivers that underpin the three key or central development risks that have been identified.

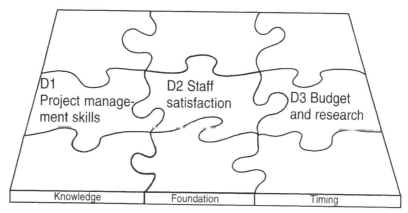

Figure 7.4 Key development drivers

7.3.1 Development drivers risk 1 - Project management skills

The drivers behind the unrealistic work estimates issue are related to a lack of understanding concerning the technological implications of the system being developed. This could be due to the use of new, leading-edge technology and new applications with which the organisation is not familiar, or having to do a rush job to respond to a crisis or perhaps there being no contingency built in to the figures or numbers. A lack of project management experience may also be responsible for poor work estimates, as might the requirement to put in a better bid than that of an outsourcer. It is sometimes said that risk averse organisations may be worse at estimating than risk tolerant ones as the risk averse firms may not be prepared to face all the difficult issues.

7.3.2 Development drivers risk 2 - Staff satisfaction

The drivers that underpin the implementers not remaining in post include unrealistic employment conditions, poor working relationships and no future vision for the staff. Key members of the development team sometimes leave the project just before its completion, which can suggest that they may not have had as much faith in the projects as they appeared to have. The drivers which affect key users moving positions within the firm are more complex, but relate to the need for the organisation to recognise the importance of the IS development and the role which some individuals play. If key users are seen as IS owners then the harmful aspects of the practice of moving individuals during IS development will be highlighted.

7.3.3 Development drivers risk 3 - Budget and research

The drivers responsible for the use of inappropriate or inadequate development tools are most likely insufficient technological experience, lack of management discipline within the IS department and poor market research or market understanding on the part of the technical people. The question of not understanding the market is often a budgetary one as it is expensive to allocate resources for market scanning.

The drivers that result in the development risks are often related to budgetary restraints. If IS development and management are funded adequately then much of this risk will be reduced.

7.4   Architecture drivers

Figure 7.5 shows three key architecture drivers underpinning the three key or central architecture risks that have been identified.

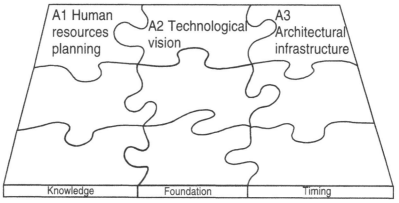

Figure 7.5 Key architecture drivers

7.4.1   Architecture drivers risk 1 - Human resources planning

The drivers associated with the organisation not having appropriate expertise to be able to successfully implement the chosen technology are very similar to those described for the previous risk above. However the following three points may also be added.

1   a naïve understanding or belief in the 'architecture';

2   no medium or long-term human resources planning;

3   a corporate vision that sees IS as a support activity that exists for record-keeping purposes, i.e. to keep the books and perhaps to help with correspondence, i.e. word processing.

7.4.2   Architecture drivers risk 2 - Technological vision

There are many different reasons why there may be inappropriate or inadequate hardware or software platforms in use. Some of these reasons are:

1   no long-term IS vision, resulting in or being the cause of, no

corporate IS or IT architecture (see Appendix E) or standards being in place;

2 no mechanism for ensuring that whatever policy there is, is being maintained;

3 no market/technology research and thus no understanding of the direction of technological advances;

4 far too big a group of, and investment in legacy systems;

5 no appreciation of the strategic potential of appropriate IS developments.

7.4.3 Architecture drivers risk 3 - Architectural infrastructure

If the organisation does not have appropriate expertise to be able to successfully implement the chosen architecture then this implies that the technology being used has not been adequately planned. Perhaps there is no overall strategy as described in the two risk drivers outlined above. However, this usually means that the organisation has been doing little or no market scanning or research so that it does not understand the current use of the technology.

There is also the issue of there being an appropriate budget to obtain and retain the correct type of personnel. Some organisations believe that their IS departments are a necessary evil and they normally try to run there IS development on a budget that is just too tight and this directly affects staffing. In a similar vein some organisations have a short-term view of IS development.

7.5 Summary

Understanding the drivers of potential problems is the key to successful IS risk management. Figure 7.6 shows the jigsaw with the full driver set. A considerable amount of time needs to be spent on reviewing why a problem may occur. This is not a trivial task and requires insight into the organisation and the relationships between key players and the political power structure of the organisation.

How and why funds are allocated to the IS function is also a key issue in studying risk drivers. But this time is well spent, as the knowledge so acquired will give the project manager the opportunity of taking action to minimise the negative impact of risks or potential problems before they arise.

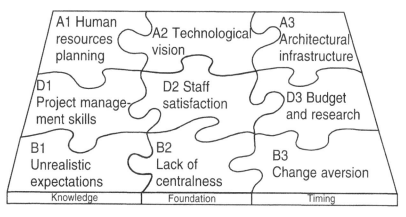

Figure 7.6 Jigsaw showing the full driver set

Key learning points in this chapter

- ❑ Risk drivers are the keys to understanding why the risks occur. Only by understanding the drivers can real action be taken to prevent or ameliorate the impact of the risk.

- ❑ The drivers of the business risks are largely to do with organisational relationships and commitment to the IS project.

- ❑ The drivers of the development risks are largely to do with funding and budgetary constraints.

- ❑ The drivers of the architecture risks are largely to do with not having spent the time and the resources understanding how information systems can support the organisation. These drivers also indicate how the organisation has not got to grips with what is happening in the IS market place and how these developments may be used by the firm.

Practical action guidelines

Create a large version of the major risk jigsaw as shown here.

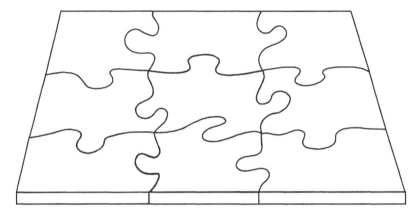

Through discussion with colleagues identify the three most important drivers of business risks, development risks and architecture risks you believe your IS project has to face. Write these risk drivers into the appropriate piece of your jigsaw diagram.

In these discussions, questions to ask include:

How do we make sure that we have captured the support of all the principal stakeholders?

What can we actively do to prevent the principal stakeholders from losing interest in the IS project?

Is our strategic information system plan adequate for all the principal stakeholders to understand and be committed to what we are trying to achieve?

8 Relationships and ripple effects

The affair was partly a lottery, though with the ultimate result largely governed by whether the abilities and character of the managers were above or below the average. Some would fail and some would succeed. But even after the event no one would know whether the average results in terms of the sums invested had exceeded, equalled or fallen short of the prevailing rate of interest; though, if we exclude the exploitation of natural resources and monopolies, it is probable that the actual average results of investments, even during periods of progress and prosperity, have disappointed the hopes that prompted them. Businessmen play a mixed game of skill and chance, the average results of which to the players are not known by those who take a hand.

(Keynes, 1964)

The only fence against the world is a thorough knowledge of it.

(Locke, 1693)

Spoon feeding in the long run teaches us nothing but the shape of the spoon.
(E.M. Forster, quoted in: *Observer* (London, 7 October 1951)

8.1 Introduction

To fully understand the role of risk in an IS project, the question needs to be addressed as to whether the risks identified are independent of each other, or whether they are actually connected or correlated in some way. This chapter discusses the issue of how risks are related and how they often have a ripple effect that can adversely influence other areas of IS project development. In general IS risk management needs to focus on those risks that have close connections and which can impact on other issues. This is the case with many IS development risks and is why the jigsaw metaphor is quite useful when thinking about them.

8.2   Relationship diagrams

It is useful to map the relationships between risks in order to have a clearer idea of how risks are linked and how they affect each other. It is also useful to note that high risk areas may easily affect low risk areas, and that careful management of the high risk areas can significantly reduce the need for risk management in other areas at a later date in the project.

The relationships between risk categories and domains differ for each organisation, both in terms of connections and the closeness or strength of the connections.   Figure 8.1 is a generic risk relationship diagram using the risk categories or taxonomy developed in Chapter 4. This diagram is a conceptual map, which provides the basis for understanding how different IS development risks can impact on one another. By using a conceptual map such as shown in Figure 8.1 a plan may be developed which can minimise or at least limit the impact of some of the risks.

It is important to note that not only are the connections between the risks significant, but also the directions of the influences described are critical, and thus should be mapped.   Some practitioners choose to depict the strength of the relationships by varying the thickness of the connecting lines, but this may be too complicated a refinement.

The probability, when operationalising the concepts described in Figure 8.1, is that virtually all of the nine issues will have some impact on all of the other eight issues. If a diagram is drawn showing this large number of connections it loses its ability to help managers focus on the most important issues. Therefore, when using a risk relationship conceptual map as shown in Figure 8.1, it is important to filter out as many of the minor, or less important issues as possible, and to focus on the relationships between the major risk categories

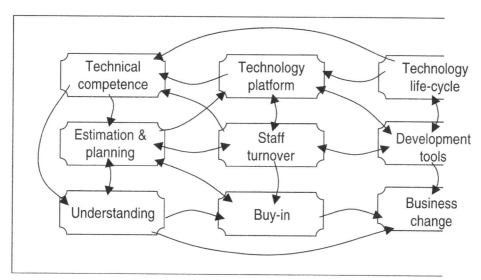

Figure 8.1 A risk relationship conceptual map

and domains that have the greatest impact on one another and on the project. Notice that only if the strength of the impact of the domains or the categories are thought to be equal should a two-directional connector line or arrow be used. Otherwise a one directional arrow pointing to the strongest impact is drawn.

8.3   Business risk relationships

In Chapter 4, three major business risks were discussed. Although these may be regarded as important risks, which could actually cause the catastrophic failure of the information systems, they are by no means the only business risks an IS development project faces. The risks described were:

1   The main stakeholders have an incomplete or inadequate understanding of the main business problem or opportunity.

2   Despite initial appearances users don't properly buy-into the proposed information system.

3   Changes that occur to the IS requirements during development are not accepted or accommodated by the development project.

If, when risk analysis is performed, it is thought that the first business risk (referred to as BR1) is a distinct threat, then in addition to preparing plans to cope with this particular risk, it is important to brainstorm how it could cause other problems or risks to arise.

Considering the example risks above it may be seen that if BR1, i.e. *the main stakeholders have an incomplete or inadequate understanding of the main business problem or opportunity*, is significant then it is quite probable that the stakeholders will not have fully bought-into the proposed information system. This *lack of buy-in or commitment* is referred to as BR2. Thus the presence of BR1 suggests the possibility of BR2 occurring, as these risks are not independent.

The rationale for this conclusion or position is simply that if the stakeholders did not fully understand the project then it is unlikely that their commitment to the project will be lasting.

Furthermore, if BR1 and BR2 are highly probable risks, then it is also probable that the *project planning and estimates*, described as risk DR1, will be inaccurate or unfounded. Inversely, poor project planning with respect to resources, finance, or people, may cause a lack of commitment to the project by the business. It is inevitable that if there is unclear understanding of the business issues, then resource allocations are likely to be difficult to secure from the business stakeholders.

In a similar way, if BR2, i.e. *despite initial appearances users don't properly buy-into the proposed information system*, is significant then it is quite probable that *changes that occur to the IS requirements during development are not accepted or are not accommodated by the IS development project*, i.e. BR3. The rationale for this position is simply that if the stakeholders did not properly buy-in to the proposed information system their tolerance for proposed changes to the requirement as the development project proceeds is likely to be rather low.

As may be seen from Figure 8.1, there is not only a correlation between BR1 and BR2, and between BR2 and BR3, but also there is a correlation between BR1 and BR3. In fact it can be quite difficult to separate these business risks and they are best managed from a holistic point of view.

Clearly there are many different possible connections between the boxes in Figure 8.1. The number of connections or the issue of the interconnections of the different risks can be seen as directly related to whether there is a comprehensive IT architecture in place. The more thoroughly the IT of the organisation has been designed the lower the possibility for IS development project failure. Of course this does not mean that even the best designed IT architecture cannot fall foul of problems, but by and large organisations who have spent the time to create strategies, to put in place standards, and to obtain stakeholder's commitment face lower IS development risk profiles.

8.4   Development risks

There is no doubt that the problem of the interdependence and the knock-on, effects of risk is extensive. For example the process of information system development links the business with the technology. Thus it is not surprising to observe that development risks are related to most other risk categories.

For instance, the consequence of poor planning and estimation will not only be felt within the development project, but will affect both the architecture and the business risks. They could easily result in the information system being built for an inappropriate technology platform. Poor planning and estimation will also affect the credibility of the project team and as a result business buy-in may suffer.

The consequence of high staff turnover is likely to be that there will be delays and also possibly a drop in standards as new staff are pressured to develop the system without an acceptable or even realistic learning curve. Thus excessive staff turnover will cause project plans and estimates to be incorrect. Business buy-in may also suffer as seasoned business users are required to re-explain processes and issues to new staff. Of course turnover in the key user community also represents a significant risk to the project.

Staff turnover also affects and is affected by the technology platform. A high turnover of staff requires the project to bring new staff into the project with the appropriate technology platform experience. There is significant risk to the stability of the IS delivery platform if staff with little experience of the technology develop the project.

If the chosen development tools do not deliver at the pace of business change, the project will lag significantly behind the business and will consistently deliver old solutions for new problems. Ease of use and stability of the development platform has a direct bearing on a mobile IS development workforce, and many cases are documented in which development staff leave a project because they are dissatisfied with the development platform. Tampoe (1993) suggests that the prime motivators of IS workers are: autonomy, or the ability to work without close supervision; growth, which in many IS professionals translates into movement with the new technology; and achievable goals, upon which the development tools and business change risk factors have direct bearing. Interestingly 'money' was found to be a prime motivator in only 7% of IS professionals. Tampoe goes on to say:

The effective management of the creative abilities of its professionals and technologists forms a cornerstone of any innovative endeavour.

8.5 Architecture risks

Architecture risks include the competence of the development team, the support and maintenance team, the choice of technology platform and the stage at which the chosen technology is in its life cycle. If the technology is too new, it may be unstable and may not be able to handle high transaction volumes. Furthermore it may be difficult to get competent or experienced staff. If the technology is near the end of its life cycle, there may also be problems in acquiring staff, or in getting support for obsolete systems. Probably the most significant risk of using old technology is the probable slowing effect it will have on the pace of business change.

A stable and widely implemented technology platform allows for better planning and estimation of development time-scales and effort required to build information systems using the technology. An established technology platform implies that one element of the staff turnover risk, namely availability of staff, will be reduced, and also that development tools will have been tried and tested for the new technology.

There can be no doubt that the competence of the project team and the subsequent maintenance team plays an important role in other risk categories. If staff have proven their competence in the technology both the understanding of the business problem and the technology's capability of providing appropriate business solutions must be enhanced, as must business buy-in to the project.

8.6   Thinking in themes or perspectives

The taxonomy of risk has the horizontal dimensions of business risks, development risks and architectural risks. It also has vertical domains that allow risk management practitioners to apply a different perspective to interconnected risks.

The horizontal dimensions of business risk have been fully discussed in Chapter 4 and it is now necessary to explore the implications of the vertical dimensions and how the performance of an IS development project may be improved by an understanding of these issues.

8.7   The knowledge perspective

The first perspective in the lefthand column of Figure 8.2 prompts questions about the knowledge within the company, or possible outsource suppliers as a source of risk. This risk perspective is different to a risk dimension in that it requires the IS development team to reflect on their own knowledge as well as the knowledge of some of their principal stakeholders. Clearly this is not an easy task.

8.7 The knowledge perspective

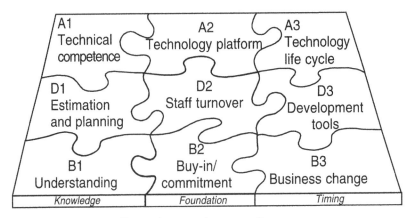

Figure 8.2 The risk jigsaw showing dimensions and perspectives

The knowledge perspective is shown separately in Figure 8.3 and consists of the three issues of understanding, estimation and planning, and technical competence.

Figure 8.3 The knowledge perspective in the risk jigsaw

The type of questions which must be answered when thinking about the organisation's and/or the project's knowledge perspective are:

1 How well do we know our business?[1]

---

[1] Of course there will always be problems with questions like this one as it is hard to envisage anyone replying that they do not actually know their business very well. Perhaps in cases such as this the role of the independent objective consultant comes into its own.

2 How confident are we that our business thinking is strategically sound?

3 How capable are our users of thinking outside of current circumstances, or will our new system merely replicate current business problems on new technology?

4 How well does the business understand different IS architectures – what it can and cannot do? How well will our business analysts understand the business problem, and can they translate this understanding into a technical solution?

5 How good are we at project management?

6 How accurate has our estimation and planning been in the past?

7 Do we have the technical competence to manage the development of the new system and of the new technology platforms?

8 If not, is outsourcing an option?

9 How knowledgeable are the prospective outsourcers?[2]

10 How knowledgeable are we about outsourcing alternatives available?

It should be remembered that this first perspective asks questions about what needs to be known concerning all the three risk dimensions, i.e. the business risks, the development risks and the technical risks. The emphasis of this enquiry is on the competencies of all parties to be involved in the development of the new information system.

8.8 The foundation perspective

The second vertical risk domain examines the foundation upon which the development project will be based.

---

[2] The knowledgeability of the prospective outsourcers may be best tested by taking references from other organisations which have used them to provide a service similar to the one which is now required.

The foundation perspective is shown separately in Figure 8.4 and consists of the three issues of buy-in/commitment, staff turnover and technology platforms.

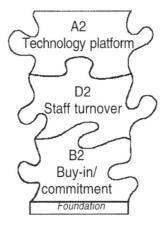

Figure 8.4 The foundation perspective in the risk jigsaw

The type of questions which must be answered when thinking about the organisation's and /or the projects foundation perspective are:

1 Do we have solid business buy-in to the change, to the disruption and to the expense that the project will inevitably occasion?

2 Is there sufficient commitment in the business to change the processes, practices and behaviours of all staff who will be directly or indirectly affected by the proposed new system?

3 How credible is the development team to the business stakeholders and other users and systems owners?

4 Do we currently have the staff on hand and the staff turnover stability to undertake such a project?

5 How are we going to encourage staff to remain in post at least until the end of the project?

6 How many critical staff are there in the project team, and what contingencies are we making to protect our interests from unreasonable staff demands or staff movements?

7 Will we reward project staff any differently in order to motivate them to achieve a successful completion of the project?

8 Do we have the correct technological platform for such a system as the one proposed?

9 How well does this technology interface with our technologies, both computer and other technologies in general?

10 How many of these foundation issues do we need to resolve for the proposed project and how many of them are actually part of the routine way in which the organisation conducts it day-to-day business?

Thus in summary the second theme or perspective asks whether the project will be based on a sound footing.

8.9   The timing perspective

The final perspective is concerned with timing related issues. The timing perspective is shown separately in Figure 8.5 and consists of the three issues of business change, development tools and technology life cycles.

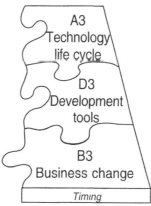

Figure 8.5 The timing perspective in the risk jigsaw

The type of questions which must be answered when thinking about the organisation's and /or the project's timing perspective are:

1   At what stage in the hardware and software and tele-communications product life cycle is the technology platform upon which we are intending to build the proposed information system?

2   Do the development tools available support the business cycle requirements – can these tools help to deliver the system in time to gain the business benefits envisioned by the project?

3   Can other development tools be acquired which can speed up the IS development life cycle?

4   Can the development tools deliver supportable, changeable code?

5   How long will it take to learn the proposed development technology?

6   Where is the business in its change cycle?

7   Will the business's change cycle interfere with the demands of the proposed project?

8   To what extent will market or people or political or technological turbulence cause shifting project goals?

9   How fast can decisions be taken by the business?

10 What are the main facilitators of change in the business and how fast can they respond when they are needed?

Thus the third theme focuses on how fast or slowly things can get done, and looks at cycles of changing technologies and business strategies.

8.10 Six ways of thinking about risk

The taxonomy of risk presented in this book serves as a conceptual model to allow risk management practitioners to picture the various dimensions of risk:

1 The business risk dimension examines risks that occur in the business environment, which affect all other risk areas.

2 In examining development risk, we are prompted to examine those risks inherent to the project environment.

3 In the technical risk dimension, practitioners look at the technology upon which the business solution is based, and the competence of the business to support that technology.

4 We look at risks related to our knowledge – of our business, within the project, and of the technology.

5 Risk is examined from the foundation upon which the IS project will be based.

6 Finally the timing and cycle issues are examined.

This may appear to some readers who are new to the issue of IS development risk to be an overly exhaustive or even exhausting approach to examining risk. However, three points should be considered:

First, the relative cost of performing this multi-perspective analysis of risk is minimal when compared to both the project cost, and the potential cost of unplanned-for consequences which occur as a result of not analysing and subsequently managing risk. If the project cost is small then the project risk is usually, but not necessarily, also small. If the risk management component is large in comparison to project size, then the risk is very high in the project and risk management is appropriate, or the time spent on risk management is excessive.

Second, the time taken to analyse risk and subsequently to manage it on an ongoing basis is similarly minimal compared to the total work effort or hours that will be finally expended on the project as a whole.

Thus in terms of these two points there is frequently a very large payback for the time and effort expended in risk management.

8.11 Summary

It is necessary for IT staff to exhibit a high degree of professionalism. There are many different and sometimes contentious definitions and descriptions of professionalism. However professionals usually conform to standards of excellence, exhibit skills and competence and earn respect. To be able to do this successfully IS professionals need to be able to mange the risks associated with the development of information systems. Ignorance of the risks that face every IS project is one of the main causes of IS development failure. There is little excuse for IS professionals not taking an active interest in this field. Managing IS risks competently will lead to there being a minimum of unplanned consequences during and after the development project.

Examining risk from different perspectives allows risk management practitioners to see risks that cannot be identified by a linear approach. As British poet W. H. Auden said:

It takes little talent to see what lies under one's nose, but a good deal of it to know which way to point that organ.

(quoted in Green, 1989)

Key learning points in this chapter

- ❑ Risks do not occur in isolation of each other. One risk affects other areas of risk and of the project.

- ❑ It is necessary to examine risks from many different perspectives in order to identify both the risk and the relationship that the risk has to other risk areas.

- ❑ While an exhaustive risk survey might appear to be long winded, the cost and time associated with such risk analysis should be minimal in comparison to the potential benefits from such an exercise. There is a large potential ROI for risk management projects.

❑ The issue of the inter-connection of the risks can be seen as directly related to whether there is an IT architecture in place.

Practical action guidelines

Draw your own risk relationship diagram and identify which risks are linked by connecting risks with arrows.

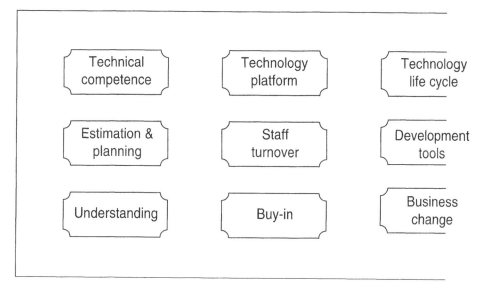

Describe what each arrow means. If one risk area is particularly critical, what will be the effects on other risk areas?

Discuss with both project and business colleagues the management actions that might be necessary to manage the risk relationships.

9 | Minimising the impact

They have focused more on being in the right technologies at the right time, being able to protect their positions, and having the best people rather than on becoming ever more efficient in their current lines of business. They believe that innovation is inevitable and manageable. They believe that managing innovation is the key to sustaining high levels of performance for their shareholders. They assume that the innovators i.e. the attackers will ultimately have the advantage, and they seek to be among those attackers, while not relinquishing the benefits of the present business which they actively defend. They know that they will face problems and go through hard times, but they are prepared to weather them. They assume that as risky as innovation is, not innovating is even riskier.

(Foster, 1986)

9.1 Introduction

For every risk there is a course of action which can minimise its impact. Sometimes there are several alternative courses of action that will reduce, or in some cases actually eliminate, the risk. It is the primary objective of IS risk management to identify these courses of action and to take the necessary steps to minimise or eradicate the risks.

The question that needs to be asked is what is the minimum action that needs to be taken to ensure that the risk has been effectively neutralised. The key issue here is cost, and only the minimum cost should be expended to remove or reduce a risk.

The total amount expended on removing or reducing a risk should never be more than the cost of the problem that could occur if the risk materialises. It is important to keep this financial rule in mind at all times as some organisations have been known to spend much more on avoiding a risk than it would have cost if the problem or difficulty had actually materialised.

The jigsaw metaphor (see Figure 9.1) is once again used here to look at possible courses of actions that could be taken if the risks described in Chapter 4 should materialise.

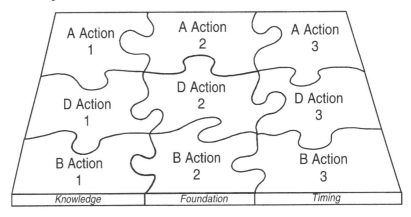

Figure 9.1 Risk action jigsaw

9.2   Business actions

The business actions shown in Figure 9.2 are examples of steps that could be taken to minimise the impact of the three key or central business risks that have been identified.

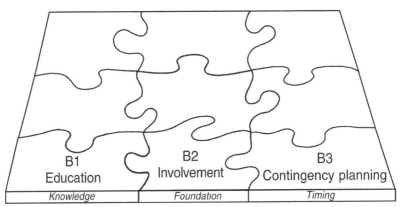

Figure 9.2 Key business actions

9.2.1 Business action 1 – Education

The action required, if it is suspected that the main stakeholders have an incomplete and inadequate understanding of the main business problem or opportunity, is to focus on the role of the stakeholders, especially the user owners of the system. This means that the IS development should be instigated by users, i.e. there should be a user system sponsor, user system owner, a user system champion and a user project chairperson.

Stakeholders importance

Understanding who the stakeholders are and engaging them in the development project is a *sine qua non* for the project to succeed. Unfortunately this is not always understood by IS project managers who sometimes see the stakeholders as just being a load of trouble.

Stakeholder involvement or commitment is a very important issue and there are no simple remedies to make sure that the IS project has the level of support which it requires. The management of stakeholders is a central issue to the success of any project and thus it is essential to understand who the stakeholders are and what their attitudes to the project are. Of course stakeholders are any individuals and groups of individuals who have a stake or an interest in a project to the extent that they can potentially have an affect on its outcome. Stakeholders can include senior management, users, financial managers, technical staff, vendors, trade unions, etc. Ideally stakeholders should be active promoters and supporters of the project, have an interest in the results and be involved in the management of the changes brought about by the project. On the other hand, stakeholders may not be active but instead play a passive role and thus have no real influence on the project at all. Sometimes stakeholders may not be supportive and in fact may be antagonistic to the IS project. In any event stakeholders can usually influence a situation, and project managers will need to be able to acquire and retain their support or minimise their antagonism wherever possible.

As part of an IS risk management programme the project manager should:

1 Identify the relevant stakeholders, pressure groups and other interested parties;

2 Assess stakeholder interests in terms of how they will react to the change brought about by the project;

3 Assess stakeholder commitment or antagonism;

4 Assess stakeholder power to promote or hinder the success of the project;

5 Promote positive stakeholder relations and attempt to ensure continued support while minimising any opposition.

This is a very challenging if not downright difficult task. One of the most important ways to influence the stakeholders is to have the IS department focus on user education as one of its central functions. In this context education refers to helping users understand how information systems can help them improve the performance of their department, function or process. In addition there is the fact that information systems may also improve their own personal performance as well.

9.2.2 Business action 2 – Involvement

No matter how positive the primary stakeholders are initially, it is possible if not likely that their enthusiasm will fade. This may be due to several reasons, one of the most common of which is that other priorities come along and dilute the original interest level.

One of the ways of trying to prevent the primary stakeholders or users' enthusiasm from fading is to ensure that they are involved with the project and playing an important role in its delivery. Thus it is important not only that users have been the project sponsors but that they are among the principal project champions. The project champions should be regularly briefed and also called upon to give support to the project as it progresses through the SDLC.

Furthermore, where possible one of the users should be at least the project chairperson if not the project manager. Where a user is performing the function of project manager this tends to keep other users interested and involved.

Of course the lapse time required for the project is also very important in sustaining the primary stakeholders' and users' interest. If the project drags out over several years then the interest level is bound to flag if not completely disappear. It is much easier to sustain interest in short projects. In the case of large projects that cannot be concluded in any period less than multiples of years, it is important to adapt a phased delivery approach and to make sure that the users are aware when each module is delivered and seen to be working. Thus big bang delivery should be avoided wherever possible.

9.2.3 Business action 3 – Contingency planning

One of the most difficult problems to come to terms with is the issue of change. This is not only an IS challenge, but is actually much more general and applies to most aspects of business and life in general. Change is often seen as threatening. Where it is not, it is seen as time-consuming and costly. It is often regard as wasteful. As mentioned earlier the term *scope creep* has been coined to ensure that information systems changes are seen to be negative.

The current approach to information management and especially the IS development arena requires a positive attitude towards continuous change. This implies that the full range of possible deliverables will probably never be completely foreseen or understood in the way they were originally envisaged at the outset of the IS project. Organisations have to be prepared to accept moving goal-posts and the resultant change as the normal way of preparing information systems.

The contingency notion or concept is one way of dealing with this problem. This states that it is not possible to be fully knowledgeable of the precise outcomes required from an information system at the outset of its development. As a result of this uncertainty, IS

The avoidance of change

The traditional IS development strategy was to avoid or at least minimise changes to the system. This approach is now generally regarded as having been a dismal failure. Thus the only way forward to a higher degree of success is to identify potential changes as early as possible and to lay down suitable plans for coping with them.

---

developers' plans can only be contingent on the current assumptions not changing. Once an assumption changes for whatever reason, the development plan must to reflect this change.

To be able to cope with this dynamic type of thinking, most organisations actually require a culture change in this respect. They need to be able to accept the inevitability of change. Organisations need to realise that the IS specification and development job is seldom ever finished (Remenyi et al, 1997).

9.3   Development actions

The development actions shown in Figure 9.3 are some examples that could be taken to minimise the impact of the three key or central development risks that have been identified.

9.3.1   Development action 1 – Project management

If it is suspected that the estimates of work were unrealistic, then the action required involves using benchmarking techniques. Benchmarking techniques for estimating work may be either internal or external. This might be as simple as obtaining a second opinion from different colleagues or associates, to producing a formal comparison using sophisticated measures of programmer and analyst productivity.

There are at least two reasons why the estimates may turn out to be wrong. The first is to do with poor workmanship on the part of the estimator. This may be fixed by either training the estimator or by

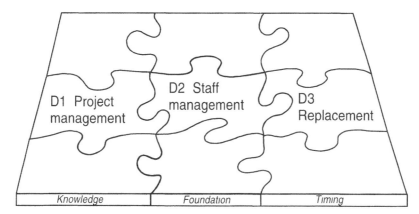

Figure 9.3 Key development actions

removing him or her from that job. The other reason why the estimates do not coincide with the actual costs is that the nature or scope of the project has changed. In this case all that is required is an update to the original estimates.

9.3.2 Development action 2 - Staff management

Like all the other risks, there are no quick and easy solutions to this problem. The actions required by IS risk management if it is believed or hinted that the implementers will not remain in post and or key users would move positions include:

1 ensuring good staff conditions;

2 ensuring people and jobs are matched;

3 ensuring there are backup arrangements for people who leave;

4 if necessary, with outsourcing contracts or arrangements.

As mentioned in Chapter 7 staff not remaining in post is often to do with remuneration and thus the action required here is in at least part, to do with appropriate funding of the IS function.

Furthermore by making sure that all IS developments have a committed user-owner and that this user-owner is involved, will also be a major help in ensuring that key user personnel stay in post.

9.3.3 Development action 3 – Replacement

The action required if it is suspected that the development tools are inappropriate or inadequate is to enhance or replace them. It is indeed folly to commence a project with development tools that will not do the job. However, a frequently encountered problem with tools is that they are not fully understood by the staff and may not be correctly applied. In such a case the provision of education is the main action required.

A simple test regarding the testing of the suitability of software development tools is to seek references from where the tools have already been put to use. This is simply another form of benchmarking which will give some assurance that the tools are appropriate.

9.4 Architecture actions

The architecture actions shown in Figure 9.4 are some examples of actions that should be taken to minimise the impact of the three key or central architecture risks that have been identified.

9.4.1 Architecture action 1 – Outsource, recruit, train

The action required if it is suspected that the organisation does not have appropriate expertise to successfully implement the chosen architecture is to take time to do a project base line study to understand the staff implication of the IS development. If such a study is not possible then the organisation should consider outsourcing or the extensive use of contractors. Of course both outsourcing and contractors may be very expensive and therefore these approaches should not be lightly embarked upon.

9.4.2 Architecture action 2 – Match

If it is suspected that inappropriate or inadequate hardware or software platforms are being proposed, make a thorough assessment of the match between the proposed platforms and what is realistically

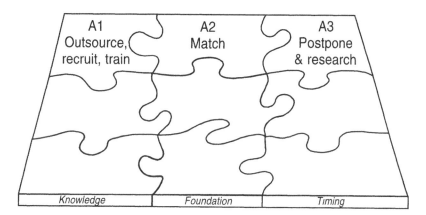

Figure 9.4 Key architecture actions

required. In this respect it clearly helps if the organisation has a corporate IT architecture in place. If it has not, then such an architecture needs to be developed as a matter of urgency. As a stopgap, a set of hardware and software standards is helpful.

However, the main action required is to delay decisions until the IS development requirements have been carefully thought through and consistent and compatible decisions are being made.

9.4.3 Architecture action 3 – Postpone and research

The action required if it is suspected that the technology is about to be leap-frogged and made redundant or obsolete, is to postpone the project until a full architecture study can be completed. Such a study should involve both internal and external benchmarking.

The risk of technological obsolesce once may be reduced by appropriate IS planning and by market and architecture scanning. It also helps if the organisation can establish hardware and software standards and also has a programme in place to continually review these standards.

9.5 Summary

There are many different ways of combating risks, some of which can be seen in the actions jigsaw shown in Figure 9.5. It is seldom possible to eliminate a risk entirely and of course there is always the possibility of something totally unexpected going wrong.

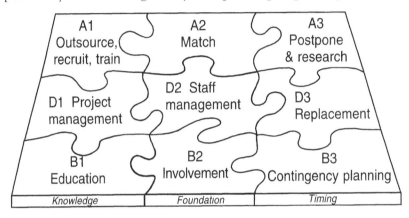

Figure 9.5 The complete actions jigsaw

In this chapter a few suggestions have been provided, many of which relate to the need to have a sound strategic IS plan and a positive attitude to the contribution that IS can make to the organisation. These are by their nature long-term issues and thus this chapter has not focused on quick fixes.

Key learning points in this chapter

❑ The total amount expended on removing or reducing a risk should never be more than the cost of the problem that could occur if the risk materialises.

❑ Stakeholder involvement is a crucial issue in IS development and it is not a simple matter to ensure that this happens.

❑ The action required to reduce business risks involves working with the project stakeholders at the outset of the project as well as over the duration of the SDLC. Furthermore, the organisation needs to be able to cope with suggestions of changes to the IS specification during the whole SDLC. There are specific methodologies for dealing with this type of situation such as active benefit realisation (Remenyi et al, 1997).

❑ The action required to reduce development risks involves working to ensure that adequate funds are available and that user-owners are and stay fully involved with the project. Benchmarking is also important in reducing the development risks.

❑ The action required to reduce architecture risks involve working to ensure that there is some degree of IS architecture in place and that appropriate staff are available, including staff who perform a technology and market research function.

Practical action guidelines

Create a large version of the course of action jigsaw as shown here.

Through discussion with colleagues identify courses of action which

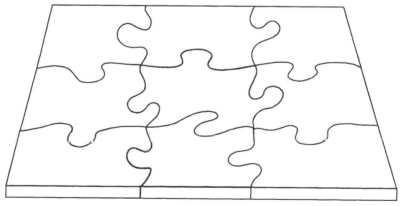

can be taken to reduce the risk exposure of the IS project. Use the jigsaw as a checklist to ensure that you have addressed all the key project risks.

In these discussions ask questions such as:

What can we do to be sure that we have fully understood the business problem or opportunity?

What can we actively do to prevent the organisation from losing any of the key members of the IS project team?

What sort of checking process can we introduce to ensure that the proposed project plan conforms with our IS architecture?

10 | Managing risk programmes

*The Law of Conservation of Information: No process of logical reasoning -
no mere act of mind or computer – programmable operation – can enlarge
the information content of the axioms and premises or observation statement
from which it proceeds.*

(Medawar, 1986)

*Any systematic efforts at project risk management must be carefully managed
if cost-effective use of risk management resources is to be achieved.*

(Chapman and Ward, 1997)

10.1 Introduction

The management of IS risk is a very challenging business which
requires considerable preparation within the organisation. It requires
the participation of both IS professionals and users, as well as any
other important stakeholders. Plans need to be put in place as early
in the SDLC as possible to ensure sound IS risk management.
However when an IS development project has already begun, it is
important not to feel that the boat has been missed. IS risk
management can be commenced at any time during the SDLC.

In fact it is often suggested that a new risk assessment should be
routinely conducted whenever anyone assumes responsibility for a
project, when there are major revisions to a plan, when a significant
deviation to a plan has taken place, when a runway situation has
occurred, or when the project moves from one stage to another.
However one of the central points of IS risk management is that it
is a reiterative process that requires continuous revisiting, reviewing
and auditing through the entire SDLC. Project success always
requires a refocusing activity and the continuous reiterative approach,
shown in Figure 10.1, ensures that risk entropy, as described in
section 3.2.2, is minimised.

10 Managing risk programmes

10.1 Introduction

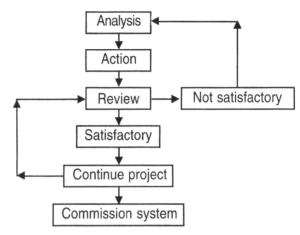

Figure 10.1 The reiterative nature of the IS risk management process

From Figure 10.1 it is clear that IS project risk management begins with an analysis process. Once this is completed a series of actions are triggered in order to reduce the risk. The original risks and the impact of these actions are reviewed from time to time. If the risk still remains too high, i.e. the situation is not satisfactory, then further analysis is required which in turn leads to more action and subsequent reviews.

If, after the review process, the risk situation is found to be satisfactory then the project manager will routinely continue with the project until the system is commissioned. However, even where the IS project risk review is found to be satisfactory, it will have to be repeated at regular periods in order to ensure that no further risk complications occur.

In this chapter an approach to operating an IS risk management process is described. The process proposed consists of seven steps:

1 appointment of a project risk management officer;

2 identify and prepare stakeholders;[1]

---

[1] The commitment of the stakeholders is central to the success of any IS project and this is especially true of its risk management aspects. Thus it is important to give adequate attention to the identification of the stakeholders and to ensure that they are properly briefed about the risk associated with the work and that they give their full backing to the risk management aspect of the project.

3 prepare and develop an IS risk management plan;

4 establish a schedule of regular risk audits or reviews;

5 where appropriate update the plan to reflect changing risks;

6 if the audit or review doesn't to lead to the plan requiring changes, continue until finished;

7 commission the project.

This approach to IS risk management is shown diagrammatically in Figure 10.2.

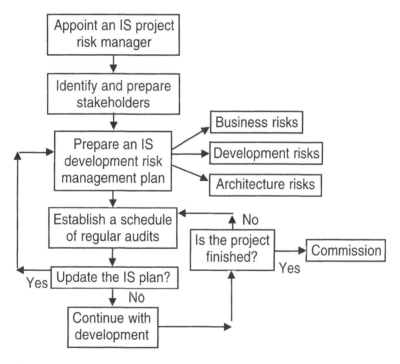

Figure 10.2 The IS risk management process

10.2 Step 1: Appoint an IS risk management officer

IS risk management requires a considerable amount of time and effort and thus for any project other than the very smallest, a risk management officer will be required. This should be an experienced individual who is familiar with both business and IS issues. If the project is quite small then the project manager or the project champion could take on the work of the IS risk management officer.

10.3 Step 2: Identify and prepare the stakeholders

At an early stage in the IS risk management process the principal stakeholders need to be identified and they need to be committed to helping identify and manage the risks. To achieve stakeholder commitment, the benefits of the risk management initiative should be clearly enunciated. This is not a trivial matter and the first step is to ensure that all the appropriate people involved with the IS development project understand the risk issue, i.e. what it is, why it is important, and what can be done to manage it. This is clearly an awareness and education exercise that will probably have to be undertaken by the IS department. It is important that the benefits of such a risk management initiative be emphasised, as staff will not take on extra work and responsibilities unless it is clear that there is some material benefit in it for them.[2]

To achieve stakeholder commitment it is sometime necessary to effect a culture change. Corporate cultures differ enormously. It is an inherent part of the corporate culture in some organisations to plan every move in the finest detail. Such organisations consider each and every aspect of a new situation and prepare estimates of all the possible contingencies they can think of. IS risk management will initially fit easily into such an organisation. The very presence of IS risk management implies that not all the project variables can be totally and accurately planned for in advance. Other organisations thrive on flexible budgeting, which attempts to accommodate a range of different circumstances. Such organisations will find it easy to work with a programme of IS risk management.

---

[2] The principal benefit which the stakeholders will derive from a IS project Risk management program is the avoidance of being involved with a failed or problematical project.

> **Changes in corporate culture**
>
> Changes in corporate culture is beyond the scope and the capabilities of most IS risk management officers. If a true corporate culture change is required then it will be necessary to set up a separate project to achieve this before a successful IS risk management programme may be introduced.

Sometimes the introduction of risk management requires a corporate culture change, which places greater emphasise on planning and thinking ahead in general. Plans buried deep in drawers are only useful to economic historians and industrial archaeologists. It is not easy to change corporate culture and thus it may take some time and effort to convince the stakeholders of the importance of undertaking a risk management programme.

10.4 Step 3: Develop a risk management plan

An IS development risk management plan is essentially a project within a project, the setting up of which requires a full understanding of all the variables concerned. This involves four phases:

1 identifying the risks;

2 establishing the consequences of the risks materialising;

3 understanding the drivers of the risks;

4 agreeing a course of action to minimise the risks.

Some consulting firms have long checklists of the problems and difficulties an IS development project could encounter and these are used as input to developing the risk management plan. Sometimes these lists are daunting and consequently they are not completed at all, or they are filled out in such haste that they do not necessarily reflect the true risk situation.

10.4.1   Identifying the risks

The approach recommended here is that a relatively small number of important IS project risks be considered in detail. These risks have been grouped under the headings of business risks, developement risks and architecture risks. This is a focusing approach which will allow an in-depth understanding of the major potential problems, and will be helpful when preparing a practical response to these risks.

A set of the more common manifestations of the business risks, which are described as business questions, is provided in Figure 10.3. This list is provided to offer the IS risk management officer a starting point from which to focus on the risks related to the central business issues. Notice there are 12 business questions which cover the three main business risks described in Chapter 4. The first group of four business questions relate to the understanding risk. The second group of five business questions relate to the buy-in/ commitment risk while the third group of three questions refer to the changes risk.

A set of the more common development risks, which are described as development questions, is provided in Figure 10.4.

Scales 1=Low and 4=High

The method of scoring the risk issues suggested here is of course subjective. It is therefore important that the criteria used to underpin this scoring be discussed by all the different individuals concerned with the management of the development project risk. Providing the same sort of thinking is used from one phase in the development project to another, there should be no problem with the fact that the risk assessment is essentially subjective. But if new individuals are introduced into the risk audit process then considerable care needs to be exerted that the same values and resultant criteria are being used.

RISK ISSUES	BR*	Acceptable risk level 1 = Low 4 = High	Assessment 1 = Low 4 = High	Gap‡
Business questions				
Is there appropriate business architecture in place and does the project make business sense?	1			
Is there a suitable degree of strategic alignment and does the project support the business strategy?	1			
Is the business problem properly understood as the project will fail or at least be delayed if not?	1			
How vulnerable is the business? If the project fails, will the business also?	1			
Is there appropriate support from the key stakeholders and is the buy-in in place?	2			
Are political and personal relationships poor, as project failure may be desirable for political reasons?	2			
Do most users see the project as advantageous and is there stakeholder support?	2			
Are users uncommitted to the changes, as the project will not deliver anything the users will use or need?	2			
Are most users located in a single geographical area, because delays can be caused by time spent communicating with users?	2			
What existing procedures will the project change, as new procedures in addition to a new system, may prove too much?	3			
Is other organisational change likely during the project and will users be able to cope with the level of change?	3			
Have mechanisms which cope with change such as formative evaluation been put in place?	3			

Figure 10.3 Some of the more common business risks

Notes: * BR = Business risks; the 1 refers to the understanding risk, the 2 refers to the buy-in/commitment risk and 3 refers to the changes risk.

‡ The gap is calculated as the difference between the risk assessment from the acceptable risk level.

10.4 Step 3: Develop a risk management plan

RISK ISSUES	DR*	Acceptable risk level 1 = Low 4 = High	Assessment 1 = Low 4 = High	Gap
Development questions				
How large is the project relative to previous ones in the organisation? If it is too big it may not be implementable.	1			
Can the project be delayed due to disputes over a poorly defined and agreed approach?	1			
Is the project dependent upon third parties whose delays can prevent delivery?	1			
Does the design need a large group, as this can lead to a project too complex to be implemented?	1			
Is a 'big bang' implementation unavoidable, as volumes of transactions and of change can be underestimated?	1			
Are the users unfamiliar with the technology, as user resistance may delay implementation?	1			
How much of the project may be outsourced, which can reduce the risk?	2			
Is the design of the project dependent on very few people, as key personnel can leave and the project fail?	2			
Are individual project roles poorly defined, which can lead to duplications, omissions and conflicts?	2			
Are staff unable to commit sufficient time to the project, as delays can occur pending time required from key staff?	2			
Are the required skills unavailable, as extra costs will be incurred acquiring the required skills?	2			
Are some staff indispensable to the project, as non-availability of key staff will directly impact delivery?	2			
Are appropriate development tools available?	3			
Are development tools compatible with each other?	3			
Is the quality of the existing data poor, as substantial data clean up impacts on time scale and/or feasibility?	3			

Figure 10.4 Some of the more common development risks

---

* DR = Development risks; the figures show how the different questions match the different risks in a similar way to Figure 10.3.

A set of the more common architecture risks, , which are described as architecture questions, is provided in Figure 10.5 below.

RISK ISSUES	AR*	Acceptable risk level 1 = Low 4 = High	Assessment 1 = Low 4 = High	Gap
Architecture questions				
Is bespoke programming a major part of the project, as such systems do not always fulfil all business requirements and/or are bug-ridden?	1			
Is there adequate competencies in the chosen technology?	1			
Is there readily available a pool of competent professionals who may be employed?	1			
Is the project technologically complex, as overcoming technical complexities causes delays?	1			
Is the technology well supported locally, as long delays for support can cause the technology to fail irreparably?	2			
Are the proposed vendors sound and what happens if they go bust?	2			
Is there a disaster recovery plan in place?	2			
Is new or untried technology being used as a fundamental part of the project, as new technology can prove impossible to use successfully in the time scale?	3			
Is unfamiliar software being used, as software bugs can delay or prevent implementation?	3			
At what stage in the product life cycle is the technology?	3			

Figure 10.5 Some of the more common architecture risks

It is not suggested that these lists are in any way definitive. Each IS development will have it own set of risks and these lists are simple baselines from which to start the risk management process. The issues listed here will need adding to in most cases. However it is also important not to create lists of hundreds of issues as these will

---

* AR = Architecture risks; the figures show how the different questions match the different risks in a similar way to Figure 10.3.

soon become incomprehensible to most individuals if not in fact to everyone. Thus the emphasis needs to be placed on balance.

These three different lists amount to an information system Project Risk Assessment Questionnaire, which will prompt an IS risk management officer to think about all the major areas of potential risks. The column in the questionnaire which is designated 1=Low and 4=High allows the potential impact of the risk on the project to be assessed on a scale of 1 to 4.

RISK ISSUES	BR	Acceptable risk level
Business questions		
Is there appropriate business architecture in place and does the project make business sense?	1	2
Is the business problem properly understood, as the project will fail or at least be delayed if the subject area is not understood?	1	1
How vulnerable is the business? If the project fails, will the business also?	1	1
Is there a suitable degree of strategic alignment and does the project support the business strategy?	1	2
Do most users see the project as advantageous and is there stakeholder support?	2	2
Are users uncommitted to the changes, as the project will not deliver anything the users will use or need?	2	2
Is there appropriate support from the key stakeholders and is the buy-in in place?	2	1
Are political and personal relationships poor, as project failure may be desirable for political reasons?	2	1
Are most users located in a single geographical area, because delays can be caused by time spent communicating with users?	2	2
Is other organisational change likely during the project and will users be able to cope with the level of change?	3	1
What existing procedures will the project change, as new procedures, in addition to a new system may prove too much?	3	1
Have mechanisms which cope with change such as formative evaluation been put in place?	3	2

Figure 10.6 Acceptable risk levels for business risks

As a first exercise the stakeholders should consider what is an acceptable level of risk for each issue. Figure 10.6 shows the business questions with an assessment of acceptable risk levels.

On completion of the acceptable risk levels for each of the three risk categories, business risks, development risks and architecture risks, the average risk level for each category can be calculated. These averages can then be used to produce a graphical presentation of the risk profile for a project. The nine-point web diagram, shown in Figure 10.7, provides a clear view of the acceptable level of risk, as perceived by the stakeholders, for the proposed information systems development project.

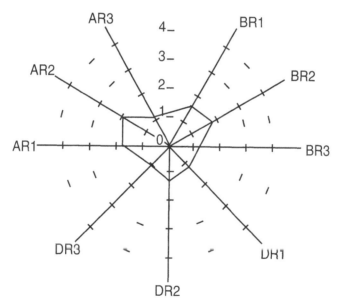

Figure 10.7 Acceptable levels of risk

The forms, which are supplied in Appendix A, can now be used to rate the actual level of risk that the stakeholders believe is present for all the issues listed in the three categories of business risks, development risks and architecture risks at the outset of the risk management programme. It is important to do this in collaboration with as many of the stakeholders as possible.

10.4 Step 3: Develop a risk management plan

It is not enough for the IS risk management officer to simply identify the risks, as it is essential to obtain the stakeholders' agreement to do something about them. This may not happen as a result of one discussion so it may be important to debate theses issues a number of times until there is a high degree of consensus.

A useful tactic in these discussions is to rank the risks and this is why the 1=Low and 4=High scale is provided. This is of course a subjective scale and may be open to some debate as to whether a specific issue deserves a particular score. However it is generally considered a useful starting point for a discussion.

The individual risk scores can also be used in an attempt to establish an overview of the total risk of the project, by averaging the scores for each category of risks. In addition, subtracting the acceptable risk level from the actual perceived risk will produce the gap. A negative gap means that the risk has been reduced to an acceptable level, whereas a positive gap implies that further risk management intervention is required.

Figure 10.8 shows a complete business risk assessment form.

This risk assessment should also be done for development risks and architecture risks.

In Figure 10.9 the business risk assessment form has been sorted in descending order by risk score. This shows where it is believed the most risk exposure for this project comes from, i.e.

1 problems due to communications due to the geographical spread of users;

2 lack of mechanisms for formative evaluation;

3 strategic alignment problems.

The average score for this set of risks is 2.58. This score, which is both higher than the mid-value of the scale from 1 to 4 (i.e. 2.5), and higher than average acceptable risk score, which is 1.5, suggests that the business risks are on the high side.

RISK ISSUES	BR	Acceptable risk level 1 = Low 4 = High	Assessment 1 = Low 4 = High	Gap
Business questions				
Is there appropriate business architecture in place and does the project make business sense?	1	2	2	0
Is there a suitable degree of strategic alignment and does the project support the business strategy?	1	2	3	1
Is the business problem properly understood as the project will fail or at least be delayed if not?	1	1	2	1
How vulnerable is the business? If the project fails, will the business also?	1	1	2	1
Is there appropriate support from the key stakeholders and is the buy-in in place?	2	1	3	2
Are political and personal relationships poor, as project failure may be desirable for political reasons?	2	1	3	2
Do most users see the project as advantageous and is there stakeholder support?	2	2	2	0
Are users uncommitted to the changes as the project will not deliver anything the users will use or need?	2	2	2	0
Are most users located in a single geographical area, because delays can be caused by time spent communicating with users?	2	2	4	2
What existing procedures will the project change, as new procedures, in addition to a new system may prove too much?	3	1	3	2
Is other organisational change likely during the project and will users be able to cope with the level of change?	3	1	1	0
Have mechanisms which cope with change such as formative evaluation been put in place?	3	2	4	2

Figure 10.8 Some of the more common business risks

RISK ISSUES	BR	Acceptable risk level 1 = Low 4 = High	Assessment 1 = Low 4 = High	Gap
Business questions				
Are most users located in a single geographical area, because delays can be caused by time spent communicating with users?	2	2	4	2
Have mechanisms which cope with change such as formative evaluation been put in place?	3	2	4	2
Is there a suitable degree of strategic alignment and does the project support the business strategy?	1	2	3	1
Is there appropriate support from the key stakeholders and is the buy-in in place?	2	1	3	2
Are political and personal relationships poor, as project failure may be desirable for political reasons?	2	1	3	2
What existing procedures will the project change, as new procedures, in addition to a new system may prove too much?	3	1	3	2
Is there appropriate business architecture in place and does the project make business sense?	1	2	2	0
Is the business problem properly understood as the project will fail or at least be delayed if not?	1	1	2	1
How vulnerable is the business? If the project fails, will the business also?	1	1	2	1
Do most users see the project as advantageous and is there stakeholder support?	2	2	2	0
Are users uncommitted to the changes, as the project will not deliver anything the users will use or need?	2	2	2	0
Is other organisational change likely during the project and will users be able to cope with the level of change?	3	1	1	0

Figure 10.9 Business risks sorted by risk assessment

On completion of the risk assessment for each of the three risk categories, business risks, development risks and architecture risks, the average risk level for each of the three sub-sections (BR1, BR2, BR3 etc.) for each risk category can be calculated. The data can then be used to produce a graphical presentation of the risk profile for a project. This nine-point graph which is shown in Figure 10.10 provides an immediate impression of the overall risk of the proposed IS development project.

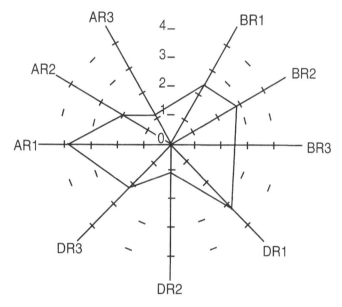

Figure 10.10 Graphical presentation of the risk profile for a project

With this type of diagram the larger the areas enclosed by the lines the great the risk profile of the project. Of course it has to be noted that in using this type of diagram as an indicator of the overall risk there is the basic assumption that the business risk, the implementation risk and the architecture risk are all of equal importance to the project.[3] As this is not likely to be the case it will probably be necessary to weight each issue.

In order to ascertain how close to the acceptable levels of risk the project is running, the two web diagrams in Figure 10.7 and 10.10 may be compared. This can be done by drawing the two sets of data

---

[3] The scoring of the different questions which underpin the three major categories of risk has been treated here on the basis that the potential problem described in each question is of equal importance. To change this assumption it is necessary to weight the questions on a scale which would reflect their relative importance.

on one common axis to produce a single web diagram. Figure 10.11 is the result, where the darker line represents the acceptable risk level.

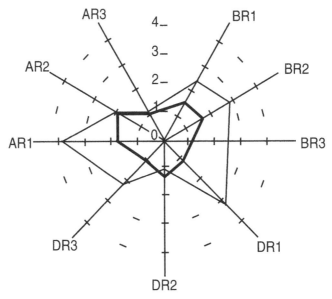

Figure 10.11 Acceptable risk levels and actual risk levels

Having completed this analysis and drawn these diagrams the IS risk management officer will be in better a position to start implementing a risk management programme.

10.4.2 Establishing the consequences of the risks materialising

Once the risks have been identified the next phase requires each category of business risks to be reviewed for a number of potential consequences or problems if the risks materialise. It is useful to rank these consequences or problems in terms of their impact on the project. As a quick rule of thumb the impact or importance of a risk can be defined as the product of its impact and the likelihood of it materialising. Of course these estimates are subjective. It is important to try to reach some level of consensus among the principle stakeholders and also check to see if the consequences or problems identified have knock-on implications for each other as the jigsaw model suggests.

This will provide a guide to the amount of effort that should be exerted to avoid the risk occurring or neutralise it. In some cases if the consequences of a problem are so severe that it may be appropriate not to proceed with the IS development project at all. In other cases the consequences will not be great and the risk may simply be accepted with the project proceeding without any further action. Most risks will lie somewhere in between these extremes.

10.4.3 Understand the drivers of the risks

Having established the consequences or the effects of the risk materialising, the next step in fully understanding the situation is to examine the drivers of the risk. There may be several drivers for each risk and an objective assessment of the importance of these drivers is essential. The drivers are the root cause of the risks and if they are correctly understood, the IS risk management officer can play a key role in preventing or avoiding the risks ever materialising.

The drivers of a risk are not always obvious and thus this activity may require considerable discussion and take up a fair amount of time. However it is only by getting to the root cause of the risks that appropriate actions can be identified. Thus it is important not to skimp on this phase of the IS risk management project.

10.4.4 Agree course of action to minimising the risks

If the drivers are correctly identified the appropriate action plans can be developed and implemented. The actions should directly attempt to affect the drivers, so that the risk will not happen. Furthermore, the actions should attempt to ameliorate the consequences if the risk does materialise.

The rule that states that the cost of avoiding a risk should be no more than the cost that will be experienced if it materialises, should be carefully borne in mind during this process. Of course a risk may have substantial intangible negative effects or soft costs, and in such cases it may be worth the organisation's while to avoid it even if the cost of avoidance appears to outweigh the cost of its occurrence.

10.5 Step 4: Establish a schedule of regular risk audits

IS risk management needs to recognise the fact that risk entropy is nearly always present in projects. Thus it is important to regularly audit or review the risk levels as well as the risk management plan. The frequency of risk reviews will be a function of the specific project, but usually project risk should be reviewed monthly or perhaps bi-monthly. If a project is regarded to be especially risky then risk reviews may be called for weekly or even more frequently. Figure 10.12 is an example of the results of a risk audit.

RISK ISSUES	BR	Assessment 1 = Low 4 = High	Risk changes	Actions required	Individual responsible
Business questions					
Is there appropriate business architecture in place and does the project make business sense?	1	1	Reduced	None	PM
Is there a suitable degree of strategic alignment and does the project support the business strategy?	1	2	No change	None	PM
Is the business problem properly understood as the project will fail or at least be delayed if not?	1	2	No change	Keep key stakeholders fully informed	Champion
How vulnerable is the business? If the project fails, will the business do so as well?	1	2	Reduced	Investigate business implications with stakeholders	PM
Is there appropriate support from the key stakeholders and is the buy-in in place?	2	3	Increased	Continue to monitor needs	PM
Are political and personal relationships poor, as project failure may be desirable for political reasons?	2	2	No change	None	PM
Do most users see the project as advantageous and is there stakeholder support?	2	3	No change	None	PM

Are users uncommitted to the changes, as the project will not deliver anything the users will use or need?	2	4	Increased	None	PM
Are most users located in a single geographical area, because delays can be caused by time spent communicating with users?	2	3	Reduced	None	PM
What existing procedures will the project change, as new procedures in addition to a new system, may prove too much?	3	1	No change	Monitor strategic development (if any)	Sponsor
Is other organisational change likely during the project and will users be able to cope with the level of change?	3	3	No change	None	PM
Have mechanisms which cope with change such as formative evaluation been put in place?	3	3	Reduced	None	PM

Figure 10.12 Results of a risk audit

10.6 Step 5: Update the plan to reflect changing risks

The result of an audit or review of a risk management plan will be to update the plan if one or more of the variables or the situation has changed. Such an update should address the same issues that have been considered in the original plan, i.e. the risks, the consequences, the drivers and the actions required.

The result of updating the project risk plans will be a second set of documents such as those shown in Figures 10.3 to 10.5 and with Figure 10.12 being a completed Risk Audit Report.

Having conducted the risk audit or review for the three risk categories, it is possible to re-sort the risk forms and to re-calculate the average risk scores for the three categories of business risks, development risks and architecture risks. This will provide an updated view of the project's risks.

The situation in the example shown here now shows an improvement in the risk profile of the project, which is even more obvious when the graphical representation of project risk is redrawn. By drawing the two sets of data on one common axis to produce a single web diagram the degree of improvement can be seen. Figure 10.13 is the result, where the darker line represents the original risk level.

Note that the average score for the set of business risks in Figure 10.2 is now 2.42 as opposed to 2.56 in the original assessment. This represents a small change for the better for this category in the risk profile to which this IS development project is exposed.

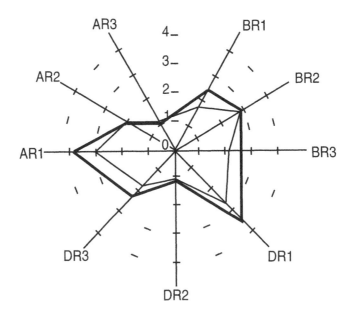

Figure 10.13 Revised representation of project risk reflecting a change in the risk

In addition to comparing the levels of risk now, with the initial levels of risk shown in Figure 10.13, merging this web diagram with the acceptable levels of risk will indicate whether the project team is succeeding in bringing the risk levels closer to the acceptable levels. Figure 10.14 shows the revised risk profile with the profile for the original acceptable risk levels. The darker line represents the acceptable risk profile.

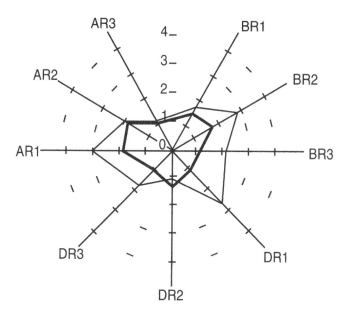

Figure 10.14 Revised risk profile compared with acceptable risk profile

As a result of the risk audit an action plan will usually need be created. Figure 10.15 shows such an action plan indicating the actions required and who has responsibility for them.

10.7 Step 6: If no changes are needed continue until finished

If plan is still on course and if there has been no material changes to any of the important risk variables then the result of the risk review may be to simply carry on as planned.

10.8 Step 7: Commission the project

The reiterative cycle of the IS risk management needs to be repeated until the IS project is finally commissioned when the whole process can be discontinued. Until the project has been commissioned the risk management programme needs to be kept active and treated in the same way as any other project. It should be run in parallel to the

10.8 Step 7: Commission the project

RISK ISSUES	Actions required	Resources required	Date for action	Individual responsible	Outcome of action
Business questions					
Is there appropriate business architecture in place and does the project make business sense?	None	None	None	PM	None
Is there a suitable degree of strategic alignment and does the project support the business strategy?	None	None	None	PM	None
Is the business problem properly understood, as the project will fail or at least be delayed if the subject area is not understood?	Keep key stakeholders fully informed	Convene a focus group	Within 15 days	Champion	Discussion paper
How vulnerable is the business? If the project fails, will the business do so as well?	Investigate implications with stakeholders	Schedule next user briefing	Within 20 days	PM	Report on business vulnerability
Is there appropriate support from the key stakeholders and is the buy-in in place?	Continue to monitor needs	Visit each stakeholder individually	Until next briefing	PM	Support shown by attending meetings
Are political and personal relation-ships poor, as project failure may be desirable for political reasons?	None	None	None	PM	None
Do most users see the project as advantageous and is there stakeholder support?	None	None	None	PM	None
Are users uncommitted to the changes, as the project delivers nothing for them?	None	None	None	PM	None
Are most users located in a single area, because delays can be caused by time spent communicating with users?	None	None	None	PM	None
What existing procedures will the project change, as new procedures in addition to a new system, may prove too much?	Monitor strategic developments (if any)	Monitor knock-on effects	Until next briefing	Sponsor	Fuller under-standing of effects
Is other organisational change likely during the project and will users be able to cope with the level of change?	None	None	None	PM	None
Are mechanisms to cope with change such as formative evaluation in place?	None	None	None	PM	None

Figure 10.15 Some possible actions required as a result of a risk audit

information system development project. The issue here is that there should be frequent risk management reviews as the risk profile and consequences of problems materialising in IS development projects are in a continual state of change.

It is never too early or too late to begin IS development risk management. The IS risk management project should ultimately be the responsibility of the IS development project manager who may delegate day-to-day operations to a competent member of staff. However final responsibility needs to be at project management level.

10.9 Summary

The management of an IS risk programme can be based on the three key risk categories or dimensions described in this chapter and earlier in the book.

It is recommended that the principle of parsimony is applied and that the risk manager focuses on a relatively small number of important issues and pays detailed attention to these.

The risk management programme can be managed in much the same way as any project as long as there are regular reviews.

Key learning points in this chapter

❑ Project success always requires a refocusing activity.

❑ Risk management takes a considerable amount of time and effort.

❑ Appoint an IS risk management officer.

❑ Stakeholder commitment is essential to sound IS risk management, and to achieve stakeholder commitment it is sometimes necessary to effect a culture change.

❑ As a general rule the cost of avoiding a risk should be no more than the cost which will be experienced if the risk materialises.

Practical action guidelines

This chapter has been based on a series of practical steps.

First:

1 appointment of a project risk management officer;

2 identify and prepare stakeholders;

3 prepare and develop an IS risk management plan;

4 establish a schedule of regular risk audits or review;

5 where appropriate update the plan to reflect changing risks;

6 if the audit or review doesn't to lead to the plan requiring changes continue until finished;

7 commission the project.

With the activity of preparing and developing an IS risk management plan there are four important phases:

1 identifying the risks;

2 establishing the consequences of the risks materialising;

3 understanding the drivers of the risks;

4 agreeing a course of action to minimising the risks.

It is important to use a questionnaire or checklist such as the example supplied in Appendix A. This helps keep focus on the crucial issues.

It is also very helpful to use diagrams to communicate the overall risk profile of the project as shown in this chapter, a template for which is supplied in Appendix A.

11 | A case study

Risky investments may indeed carry a 'premium' reward but the existence of a precise relationship between the two cannot be demonstrated or verified as there is no objective and generally accepted method of evaluating risk.

(Boyadjian and Warren, 1987)

Profits are due not to risk, but to superior skill in taking risks. They are not subtracted from the gains of labour but are earned, in the same sense in which the wages of skilled labour are earned.

(Frank A. Felice, quoted in Boyadjian and Warren, 1987)

The case of Keepers Bank International plc: A question of risk

11.1 Introduction

This case study describes how the Keepers Bank International plc reengineered a branch in order to solve an operational and financial problem and to show the way to the rest of the organisation as to how retail banking should be conducted today and in the future. This reengineering exercise required the reorganisation of a traditional branch as well as the application of the bank's information technology resources in a novel way. This new approach to retail banking is referred to as Banking 2000. Keepers has approximately 550 branches, 300 agencies and employs approximately 30,000 staff members. The bank's declared strategy is to be a bank for all the people and to supply a full range of banking services through a single delivery channel.

This case study contain numerous project risk issues, most of which were not addressed by the executives of Keeper Bank.

After the circumstances of the case is described a critique of the IS risk management is provided.

11.2 Background

Traditionally banking was based around a well-understood paradigm, which has been described in a somewhat jocular fashion by the bank's general manager of information technology Craig Balkin, as the 3–6–3 rule. The 3–6–3 rule means that bankers should borrow money at 3%, lend the money at 6% and be on the golf course by three o'clock in the afternoon. In reality the bank's ability to make the profit it requires on the margin between what it pays to its depositors and what it earns on its advances has been under severe pressure for years. This is because there is now a much smarter investor looking for the maximum return on funds, and a sharper borrower seeking the lowest interest rate available. The result is that the cost of lending is no longer as inexpensive for banks as it used to be. In addition the cost of supporting a large network of branches and agencies had become increasingly expensive.

11.3 A change in direction

Although the interest turn of the bank is still a most important contributor to its profitability, non-interest income, earned from services the bank provide, has become increasingly significant. This may be seen from Figure 11.1, which shows the relative value of these two income streams to Keepers over the past 3 years.

Year	Interest generated income (£m)	%	Non-interest generated income (£m)	%
1996	1954.6	59.97	1304.5	40.02
1997	2280.0	59.59	1545.9	40.41
1998	2593.2	56.46	1999.6	43.54

Figure 11.1: Relative value of interest against non-interest bearing income

By the mid-1990s changes in the bank's client portfolio and an increase in service demands impacted on Keepers to such an extent that some of the bank's seven regions were no longer earning the required corporate return on the funds invested in them.

11.4   Catalysts for change and key change issues

In 1996 Brian Hawkes, became general manager of the bank's largest region. Hawkes is a dynamic manager who does not believe in incremental change, but in quantum leaps, and he immediately set about the creation of a novel vision of future banking which he communicated throughout his region. Being realistic, Hawkes' timeframe for his vision to become reality in his region was five years. He began by setting a number of management development projects in motion to achieve his new banking or branch of the future vision. The most important of these were:

11.4.1   Leadership focus

One of the urgent problems Hawkes faced was an unacceptable level of staff turnover. By 1996 his region employed 3000 staff and was experiencing an annual staff turnover of nearly 1 in 4. Having closely analysed the situation it became evident that branches managed by individuals who were achievement orientated and who showed aptitude for leadership, were retaining their staff while the others were losing them. Thus Hawkes focused on a programme of leadership development and achievement orientation for critical individuals in his region. It was intended that this training would influence much of the changes that were to follow.

11.4.2   Sales focus

As business success is usually achieved through the attainment of more revenue Hawkes emphasised the need for a better level of selling skills in the region. This was impressed on the region through a series of workshops and extensive communication to attain a quantum leap in sales, therefore attaining the infrastructure's 'critical mass' of business. To emphasise the importance of his initiatives, Hawkes made sure they were perceived as being urgent by personally stressing to his management the need to build this attitude into all aspects of everyone's jobs. He coined the phrase 'energised' which is followed throughout the region.

11.4.3 Restructuring the of traditional branch

Prior to Hawkes' arrival as general manager, a typical branch in the region had seven or eight hierarchical levels of staff. Hawkes was aware that this often detracted from the client focus, which he felt was essential to the function of the branch of the future. As a consequence he introduced a new approach of branch organisation which he refers to as the *value chain model*. Branch organisation before and after these changes is shown in Figure 11.2.

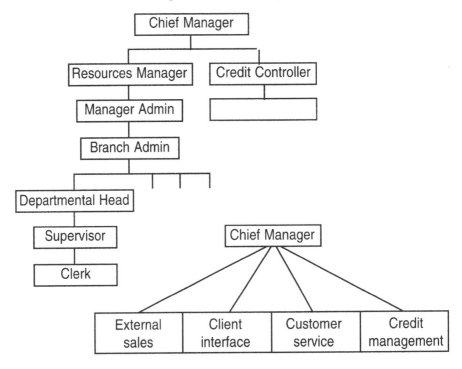

Figure 11.2 Branch organisation after implementation of the value chain model

The result was a flatter structure where the best branches now have only three levels of staff. It also reduced bureaucratic management posts. The front line chief manager in a branch can now have as many as 21 individuals reporting to him or her, giving him or her a much greater awareness of what is actually happening in the branch. The reorganisation also resulted in more direct reports to Hawkes personally at the Regional Head Office with 45 people reporting directly to him. This new structure is referred to by the bank as the value chain model.

Hawkes strongly believed the bank's branches should be managed in terms of some of the principles of general retailing. This is reflected in his desire to see greater customer interface, use of the space available in all the branches, and his notion that the bank's resources should be measured in terms of their ability to generate revenue and profit. Hawkes is committed to the notion that little can be achieved by incremental change and thus he placed considerable store on the notion of a quantum leap being the way to ensure business success. Marginal or incremental change frequently leads to temporary change, which can be relatively easily reversed when the project has been completed.

11.4.4 The information technology dimension

Craig Balkin, the General Manager of IT at Keepers joined the bank in 1985. Traditionally the Keepers Bank has had mixed fortune with its information technology policy. However in the past few years it has rectified many of its problems and Balkin was appointed to assist even more. He had immediately become champion of the use of information technology, not only to maximise the organisation's efficiency and effectiveness, but also to gain a competitive advantage. Coincidentally, Balkin had initiated, in another part of Keepers, a separate branch of the future project. His initiative started in 1997 with the objective of using the bank's enormous investment in an information technology infrastructure, as well as its substantial technological expertise and experience, to gain further competitive advantage. The aim was to create a strategic information system that would deliver a shopping-centre-wide client server system providing benefits to both merchants and customers within a shopping complex. This would enable the bank to more completely service existing merchants and thus ensure their continued custom as well as attract new business.

11.5 Balkin's and Hawkes' visions

Hawkes expressed his vision of what he could achieve by reengineering his region:

to significantly improve the performance of my region while ensuring that the service delivered to both personal and corporate clients is enhanced by reorganising the way a branch functions.

According to members of the project team, Hawkes' vision was not always readily accepted throughout the bank. On many occasions his personality was pitted against the bank's management establishment and it was only his tough-minded conviction that the branch of the future was the only way forwards that ensured the continuation of the project.

Central to Balkin's vision was to use Keepers' established large-scale information technology and backbone data and telecommunications network to provide a value-added service to customers. At the heart of this vision was the belief that the bank's information technology infrastructure could be leveraged to provide a real payoff. Keepers' infrastructure requires enormous investment and is not always perceived as delivering an adequate return. This view supported the notion of using the established investment and expertise to gain a further competitive advantage over the other banks. It was the combination of these two quite different visions, which combine information technology and management, may be seen as one of the major contributing factors to the success of the branch of the future project.

11.6 The decision

The decision to commit large resources to this project was not undertaken without considerable thought and analysis. The slow deterioration in performance over the previous years meant that the returns required to satisfy the bank's stakeholders would not be available unless a direct intervention was undertaken to reduce costs and to increase revenue. Hawkes had been thorough with his homework and had considered a number of alternatives to achieve his objectives. These included creating additional banking outlets, upgrading existing premises or implementing the branch of the future project. Clearly the first two options would be costly and would not address the underlying problems of productivity and return on investment faced by Keepers. Neither amounted to a new strategic direction which the bank felt it needed in relation to its branch network. Thus the branch of the future project was eventually chosen as the best option because it was anticipated that by changing processes and supporting staff with technology, customer service could be radically improved. Although this option was clearly also going to be expensive, it was anticipated that with the increased customer throughput, substantial economies of scale could be achieved and this would have the required effect on the profit and the return on investment.

11.7 Starting the project

Once Hawkes had committed himself to the branch of the future option, he formalised a clear mandate, albeit different from the initial one proposed by Balkin, with the objectives of:

- creating a high technology value chain environment model;

- improving customer service;

- providing a quantum leap improvement in queue management;

- facilitating excellent financial performance;

- expediting outstanding volume growth;

- allowing for a reduction in staff numbers;

- permitting a number of best practices identified to be implemented;

- fielding a physical redesign that is state-of-the art.

Hawkes divided the project into two phases, Phase one would run from January 1997 to March 1998 and would concentrate mainly on direct customer interfaces, as it was agreed this was the area where most impact could be made. The second phase would begin in October 1998 and will concentrate on re-engineering branch processes using enabling technologies such as image processing and office automation.

11.8   A pilot site

After considerable deliberation it was decided to choose a Keepers branch located in a major shopping centre called Riverwalk as a pilot site. It was intended that this project could be complete quickly and that the lesson learnt from this pilot site could be incorporated into future locations. Riverwalk is a well established shopping centre dating back to 1986, located in a moderately populated area of middle to high income families. There are more than 100 shops in Riverwalk, including major grocery chains, fashion stores, discount shops, boutiques, restaurants and fast food outlets drawing many tens of thousands of shoppers each week. Several different banks are represented. The centre was about to embark on a major modernisation programme and the Keepers branch would have to invest in updating its customer image in any case. Another key reason for this branch being selected as a suitable test site for the ideas of the branch of the future was because it was perceived as being a very average branch and therefore if the new system worked there it would probably work elsewhere just as well.

11.9   The branch of the future

The branch of the future will look and feel quite different to the branches in the current bank network and so a number of major alterations were made to the physical layout.

11.9.1 Physical layout

Underlying the design of the branch of the future is the need to optimise the utilisation of very expensive office and shop space. Traditionally a branch uses 70% of its space for backroom paper processing and 30% of its space for the client interface. As the cost of high street office and shop space has been escalating at 10% to 20% over the past decade, these proportions are now regarded as not being optimal. The backroom operations need to be conducted is a smaller area giving more space for the real business of the bank which is serving clients. This is one of the key objectives of the branch of the future project.

The first major change was the removal of cash from the front of the branch. This was achieved by the implementation of a substantial amount of technology including the teller cash dispenser (TCD) and the customer details imaging system. The TCD resulted in the security glass traditionally found in the bank's branches being removed from in front of the teller's workstation. This allowed the teller's role to change from that of handling monetary transactions to that of a multi-skilled service consultant. In the branch of the future, when clients wish to deposit cash and cheques the money is accepted by the service consultant and after being checked it is inserted in a chute which carries it to a vault away from the customer access area. When a client requires cash the service consultant uses the TCD which performs a similar role to an automatic teller machine to extract the correct amount of cash. Thus effectively the service consultant is not in possession of any cash except a few coins which are kept to make up odd amounts a client may require, for example, when it is necessary to cash a cheque for £151.56.

As a result of this, the bullet-proof glass of the tellers was removed and the tellers' counter was lowered and chairs provided. As customers' needs could be met by one multi-skilled individual, the customer would not be required to move from one individual bank employee to another who would deal with specific issues. It was therefore expected that although a customer might spend a longer period of time with a single service consultant, overall they would spend less time in the branch. Other physical layout changes included easily accessible customer interview cubicles, staffed by specialists and supported by sophisticated IT systems to deal with more intricate customer requirements. A central open information desk or cubicle which acts as a customer enquiries counter was introduced. This is not the traditional post which dealt with account queries, but is used to direct customers to the appropriate area of the branch. In addition, this cubicle acts as a promotional and sales office for affiliated products such as airline ticket purchases and cellular telephone sales. It was also proposed that the branch of the future should have a shop-like front window where Keepers' products are displayed.

On completion of Phase 1 the physical layout of the branch had changed dramatically, whereby approximately 53% of the branch space is occupied by bank staff and 47% of the space utilised by the client interface functions. Although this is a considerable improvement on the traditional space utilisation position, it is still believed in the bank, that there is room for more improvement.

11.10 The information technology

The information technology philosophy underpinning the branch of the future project was to use well-established and proven technology in an innovative way to support the major changes required. It is generally accepted that information technology is the enabler for business process reengineering, and this has played a central role in the branch of the future project. Although many alternatives were investigated with respect to peripheral hardware and support software, the Keepers' networks and their operating system were assumed to be the basic standard required. This standard was insisted upon because the bank did not wish to deviate from its communications network technology base that was uniform throughout all its branches. In addition, an important objective of its technology selection was re-usability and ease of implementation in other areas when the project was successful. The main information system used to create the branch of the future may be considered under three headings. These are the automation of the client interface process, the automation of the client support services and the factory or backroom operation.

11.10.1 The client interface process

This refers to how the service consultant works with the client and involves four key systems which are, branch automation, teller cash dispensers, a customer details imaging system, and the cross-selling system.

Branch automation

The backbone technology of the branch is a client server system comprising a Pentium II fileserver and 22 similar workstations. Of these workstations, 14 are available to the tellers and they each have a peripheral called a 'toaster' (as it looks like one) which can read the magnetic ink character recognition (MICR) details on a cheque, read, and where applicable, write to a smartcard or magstripe, and record images documents.

The teller cash dispenser (TCD)

The TCD device dispenses cash, and has a separate compartment for the acceptance of deposits. As a result the teller no longer needs to count cash that is dispensed to the customer and the TCD has reduced tellers' differences by a factor of 28 times from March 1997 to March 1998.

Customer details imaging system

This system operates on a Windows NT platform and generates images of a customer's identification and signature for tellers and supervisors which can be viewed when certain transactions or events occur. The Riverwalk branch has 20,000 accounts of which approximately 40% hold supportive documentation relating to additional signing powers, etc. It is obvious that where a number of accounts are held by the same customer, an image of their identification document as well as a customer signature card need only be held once. Time savings on accessing a signature card have reduced from an average of five minutes for a manual search to five seconds on-line.

Cross-selling system

This application is a rule-based system specifically designed to facilitate cross-selling opportunities when certain circumstances occur. For example, if a pensioner wishes to deposit a large sum the system would suggest that the customer should rather open a savings account where he or she would earn better interest, and the Bank would benefit by being able to charge the customer for utilisation of an additional account.

11.10.2 Client support services

These systems are designed to help clients obtain information about the bank's services without having to meet with several members of staff. The branch of the future provides a number of self-service devices which are high resolution, colour, interactive, touch screens, with sound capability. They are simple to operate, as they 'talk' the customer through the system. They provide product information, give estimates on loans and the purchasing of shares, request a visit from a product specialist or link existing accounts.

11.10.3 The factory operations

This refers to the automation of reporting systems that the bank needs, to retain up-to-date information about the arrangements clients have with them. Such automation can greatly reduce the amount of paper and procedures previously required to maintain this important information. An example is on-line automation of excess notices (a report produced when a customer is over his arrangements with the Bank). The piloting of this process has reduced the time needed for the production of new reports from five days to one day. It has reduced the number of actions from 29 steps to 9. This has the potential of massive savings in highcost manpower, as credit managers could be centralised in a 'warehouse' type operation.

11.11 Process identification

Phase 1 of the project, which ended in March 1998, concentrated on the client interface which is the front line of the branch. In terms of the activities directly associated with the clients, 46 branch processes were identified and mapped and five key workflows on the front line were re-engineered. For example, the opening account procedures efficiency was improved by 64% with a reduction in activities from 71 to 25. The work involved in the identification of these processes was conducted by internal staff supported by consultants.

11.12 Human resource issues

The management function for the value chain model put forward by Hawkes required a team-based management development approach. Re-learning was difficult for the management team and it was very apparent to the project team that the problems of the culture change could not be underestimated. Two of the five original managers at the Riverwalk branch have requested a transfer to other branches and in general the staff at the pioneering branch did not rush to embrace the new arrangements. However as the project proceeded the benefits of the branch of the future slowly proved themselves and today it is regarded by some of those individuals who stayed involved, as a great improvement. Everyone does of course, not share this view and there have been suggestions that branch management was not fully briefed, not to mention committed, to the change programme.

11.13 Costs of the branch of the future

Figure 11.3 gives details of actual against anticipated direct costs while the indirect costs are also shown in Figure 11.4. The investment amount for the existing branch automation LAN and its peripherals are not included in these figures as all branches are supplied with this platform. The approximate cost of this is £700K.

DIRECT PROJECT COSTS				
Division responsible	Category of cost	Budget amount (£)	Actual amount (£)	Percentage variance
ISD	New technology	189,634	197,328	–4.06
Premises division	Physical layout	1,069,000	1,330,000	–24.42
Regional head office	Reengineered rules	50,000	54,941	–9.88
Group training division	Human resource issues	30,000	31,400	–4.67
Marketing division	Marketing issues	167,600	123,145	26.52
TOTAL		1,506,234	1,736,814	–15.31

Figure 11.3 Direct project costs

INDIRECT PROJECT COSTS		
Division responsible	Category of cost	Actual amount (£)
ISD and systems and support	Project implementation	366,688
Regional head office	Front line support	25,760
ISD	Development	165,215
TOTAL		557,663

Figure 11.4 Indirect project costs

11.14 The return on investment

It is at present difficult to attribute the growth in the business and the profit experienced by the Riverwalk branch solely to the branch of the future initiatives. However, on interviewing the management of the branch, including one whose sole responsibility is obtaining business (it would be easy for him to discredit the system in an attempt to claim credit for the growth) they unanimously agreed that the branch of the future was a major contributor to the growth. The Business Development manager stated that '*the new arrangement turns all of our 10 service specialists (ex tellers) into salespersons.*'

Figure 11.5 provides some key indicators showing growth in value. The number of current accounts (net) introduced to the Bank's books grew from 200 in 1997 to 1200 in 1998.

GROWTH STATISTICS (VALUE)	
Category or Product	**1998 comparison against 1997 (%)**
Total lendings (nett)	22.70
Current a ccounts	29.60
Total deposits (Savings)	24.00
Irrecoverables (shortages)	(164.70)
Home Loans	26/80

Figure 11.5 Growth in value

From Figure 11.6 it may be seen that the branch experienced a growth rate in excess of 100.07% in profit in the first financial year in which the branch of the future had been implemented. This should be compared to a 4% from the previous year.

Comparison	%
1995/1996	N/A
1996/1997	17.05
1997/1998	100.07

Figure 11.6 Percentage annual growth

11.15 The way forward

With the success of Riverwalk, the branch of the future is being considered for being rolled out to other branches in Hawkes' region. As soon as a branch is due for refurbishment it is eligible to be re-equipped and rearranged to comply with the branch of the future. In addition, other Regional General Managers are now, under the guidance of Hawkes, beginning to consider the establishment of the branches of the future. Certain elements of the Riverwalk model with regards best practices, teller assistants, multi-skilling and the value chain model are already being seen to be appropriate, not only in the shopping centre environment, but for full-service branch environments. However to day only a very small number of branches have actually gone ahead with the bank of the future model and it clear that there is some concern among line managers about Hawkes' new approach.

11.16 Project risk management in Keepers Bank

At the initial post-implementation reviews, this IS project was regarded by the principal stakeholders at Keepers Bank plc to have been a great success. And indeed it was. The project had produced a clear improvement in performance and had received, at least to some extent the approbation of the clients and staff. However the case study described above is really only the first phase is what is hoped by the principal stakeholders to be a very much bigger IS development project and thus there is the question of how the organisation can or should proceed from this point onwards. Thus this has to been seem as having a potential conflict between short-term goals and objectives, i.e. what happens at the pilot site and long-term goals and objectives, i.e. what happens in the rest of the organisation.

11.16.1 Attitude to risk

Like many organisations, the Keepers Bank IS project development team was largely oblivious to the issue of risk. They developed what they considered to be a good idea and they pursued this as vigorously as they could. Although the project was largely successful there are several risk issues which remained present throughout the project and which actually intensified when the project was to be rolled out in other parts of the organisation.

11.16.2 Business risks

The Keepers Bank project had the fully committed support of a senior line manager and the head of the IS function within the bank. Clearly these were two extremely important stakeholders. However it did not have the same high degree of support from the individuals who would actually use the technology in the branch at the bank. This was unfortunate, as it meant that despite the hype that the organisation generated to support the project, there were more than a few individuals who did not see its great advantage to them. Some of these individuals left the employment of the bank.

It is also interesting to note that the bank did not thoroughly canvass their clients' opinion whether they would prefer to bank in the new branch environment. There are mixed views on this issue, with some clients feeling exposed in these new non-traditional banking halls.

Although the project retained the committed support of the two major stakeholders during its development and commissioning at the Riverwalk branch, it is very noticeable that this new approach to branch banking was not rapidly rolled out to other branches. In fact at the date of writing the case study, only a small handful of the 550 branches have adopted this new information-systems-based approach to banking.

11.16.3 Development risks

This IS implementation at Keepers Bank did not pose any special development risks. Keepers Bank has a highly experienced cadre of considerably more than 1000 IS professionals. It is well experienced in estimating the work involved and it has a large range of tried and trusted development tools at its disposal.

11.16.4 Architecture risks

The majority of the technology employed in the Keepers Bank information systems, including the telecommunication networks, has been tried and tested in the bank environment for some years.

There was only one new technological dimension to this project and that was to do with the optical character reading devices that were to be installed at the branch. The bank was aware of the risks associated with this technology and they ensured that they employed well-tested technology in this arena.

Using the tools and techniques described in Chapter 10 it is desirable to initiate an IS risk management plan before continuing with the project. The first step in this process is to perform a risk analysis. This may be conducted using the risk assessment forms supplied in Appendix A. The forms describing the business, development and architecture risks, and the gaps, are completed and shown in Figures 11.7 to 11.9. When the scores for the three sets of risks (the nine diferent risks in all) are averaged and plotted on a graph they appear as shown in Figure 11.10.

From the analysis it is clear that the business aspects of this project carry the real risks. If the organisation can control the business issues then this project should be achieved without any real difficulty.

11.17 Risk management issues

The risks faced by Keepers Bank International plc in their attempts to role out their vision of the bank, or the branch of the future, are very largely impacted on by business issues. It is therefore essential that they place as much attention on this aspect of the IS development.

What particular actions need to be taken depends upon the nature of the individuals involved in the project as well as their specific relationships. However in general it can be said that the branch of the future project needs to be re-sold to line management at the branch level. It also needs to be re-sold to the client base if it is to proceed.

These issues are so fundamental to a projects such as this that it is probably worth Keepers Bank International plc time to re-evaluate this project *ab initio*.

RISK ISSUES	BR	Acceptable risk level 1 = Low 4 = High	Assessment 1 = Low 4 = High	Gap*
Business questions				
Is there appropriate business architecture in place and does the project make business sense?	1	1	3	2
Is there a suitable degree of strategic alignment and does the project support the business strategy?	1	2	3	1
Is the business problem properly understood, as the project will fail or at least be delayed if not?	1	2	2	0
How vulnerable is the business? If the project fails, will the business also?	1	1	2	1
Is there appropriate support from the key stakeholders and is the buy-in in place?	2	1	2	1
Are political and personal relationships poor, as project failure may be desirable for political reasons?	2	1	1	0
Do most users see the project as advantageous and is there stakeholder support?	2	2	3	1
Are users uncommitted to the changes, as the project will not deliver anything the users will use or need?	2	2	4	2
Are most users located in a single geographical area, because delays can be caused by time spent communicating with users?	2	1	4	3
What existing procedures will the project change, as new procedures in addition to a new system, may prove too much?	3	2	2	0
Is other organisational change likely during the project and will users be able to cope with the level of change?	3	2	1	−1
Have mechanisms which cope with change such as formative evaluation been put in place?	3	1	4	3

Figure 11.7 The evaluation of the business risks

Note: * The gap is calculated by subtracting the risk assessment from the acceptable risk level.

11.17 Risk management issues

RISK ISSUES	DR	Acceptable risk level 1 = Low 4 = High	Assessment 1 = Low 4 = High	Gap
Development questions				
How large is the project relative to previous ones in the organisation? If it is too big it may not be implementable.	1	1	2	1
Can the project be delayed due to disputes over a poorly defined and agreed approach?	1	2	2	0
Is the project dependent upon third parties whose delays can prevent delivery?	1	2	3	1
Does the design need a large group, as this can lead to a project too complex to be implemented?	1	2	2	0
Is a 'big bang' implementation unavoidable, as volumes of transactions and of change can be underestimated?	1	1	1	0
Are the users unfamiliar with the technology, as user resistance may delay implementation?	1	1	1	0
How much of the project may be outsourced, which can reduce the risk?	2	2	1	−1
Is the design of the project dependent on very few people, as key personnel can leave and the project fail?	2	2	3	1
Are individual project roles poorly defined, which can lead to duplications, omissions and conflicts?	2	1	1	0
Are staff unable to commit sufficient time to the project, as delays can occur pending time required from key staff?	2	2	2	0
Are the required skills unavailable, as extra costs will be incurred acquiring the required skills?	2	2	3	1
Are some staff indispensable to the project, as non-availability of key staff will directly impact delivery?	2	1	2	−1
Are appropriate development tools available?	3	2	1	−1
Are development tools compatible with each other?	3	2	1	−1
Is the quality of the existing data poor, as substantial data clean up impacts time scale and/or feasibility?	3	2	2	0

Figure 11.8 The evaluation of the development risks

RISK ISSUES	AR	Acceptable risk level 1 = Low 4 = High	Assessment 1 = Low 4 = High	Gap
Architecture questions				
Is bespoke programming a major part of the project, as such systems do not always fulfil all business requirements and/or are bug-ridden?	1	1	1	0
Is there adequate competencies in the chosen technology?	1	2	3	1
Is there readily available a pool of competent professionals who may be employed?	1	2	3	1
Is the project technologically complex, as overcoming technical complexities causes delays?	1	2	2	0
Is the technology well supported locally, as long delays for support can cause the technology to fail irreparably?	2	1	3	−2
Are the proposed vendors sound and what happens if they go bust?	2	1	1	0
Is there a disaster recovery plan in place?	2	2	4	−2
Is new or untried technology being used as a fundamental part of the project, as new technology can prove impossible to use successfully in the time scale?	3	2	1	−1
Is unfamiliar software being used, as software bugs can delay or prevent implementation?	3	2	3	1
At what stage in the product life cycle is the technology?	3	2	2	0

Figure 11.9 The evaluation of the architecture risks

11.17 Risk management issues

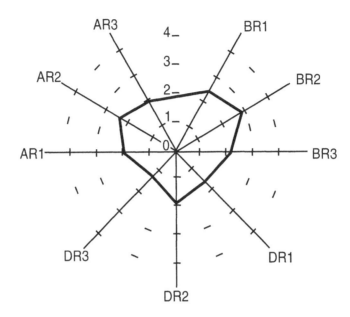

Figure 11.10 Graphical presentation of the risk profile for a project

On the positive side, the above analysis makes it very clear that the bank has all the skills and technology needed to make such a project succeed provided the stakeholders are committed to its success.

Figure 11.11 shows some possible actions required as a result of a risk audit and who would be responsible for these actions.

RISK ISSUES	Actions required	Individual responsible
Business issues		
What existing procedures will the project change, as new procedures as well as a new system may prove too much?	Re-sell to stakeholders	Sponsor
Are political and personal relationships poor, as project failure may be desirable for political reasons?	Re-sell to stakeholders	Sponsor
Is there appropriate support from the key stakeholders and is the buy-in in place?	Keep key s/h fully informed	Sponsor
Are users uncommitted to the changes, as the project will not deliver anything the users will use or need?	Re-sell to users	PM
Is other organisational change likely during the project and will users be able to cope with the level of change?	Continue to monitor users' needs	PM
Is there appropriate business architecture in place and does the project make business sense?	None	PM
Do most users see the project as advantageous and is there stakeholder support?	None	Champion
How vulnerable is the business? If the project fails, will the business also?	None	PM
Is the business problem properly understood, as the project will fail or be delayed if the subject area is not understood?	None	PM
Is there a suitable degree of strategic alignment and does the project support the business strategy?	Monitor strategic developments if any	Sponsor
Are most users located in one geographical area, as delays can be caused by time spent communicating with users?	Create a detailed roll out plan	PM

Figure 11.11 Some possible actions required as a result of a risk audit

11.18 Summary

Although no specific IS risk management was employed by Keepers Bank for this project, as it is a very well established traditional bank, their approach to IS development generally avoids risk where possible. This is clearly seen in discussing both the implementation risks and the architecture risks the project could have faced. However large, traditional, well-established banks can be exposed to substantial business risks and this is clearly evidenced in the above example. Although the two senior members of the executive management team were able to drive this prototyping project through to a successful conclusion they were not able to roll it out to all the other branches in the way they had originally envisaged. This is because they were not able to get all the stakeholders committed in the way that is necessary to ensure the eventual success of a large-scale project such as this. Simply, they did not give sufficient attention to the most important risk elements, i.e. the business risks. As a result only the prototype location for this project was a success.

Key learning points in this chapter

- ❑ IS risk management needs to be an integrated part of project management.

- ❑ IS risk management may be commenced at any time.

- ❑ Business risks are among the most difficult to identify and to manage.

- ❑ Commitment should be obtained from as wide a network of stakeholder as possible.

- ❑ The project's ultimate goals and objects need to be taken into account rather than any short-term goal or objectives.

Practical action guidelines

Ensure that you understand the goals and objectives of the project, especially if it has already begun.

Make sure that if there are any differences between short-term, medium-term and long-term goals and objects they are made clear.

Start IS risk management at whatever stage you get involved in a project.

Use the forms and diagrams supplied in this book to help you focus on the key risk issues.

12 Starting an IS risk management programme

We regard the photograph, the picture on our wall, as the object itself (the man, landscape, and so on) depicted there. This need not have been so. We could easily imagine people who did not have this relation to such pictures. Who, for example, would be repelled by photographs, because a face without color and even perhaps a face in reduced proportions struck them as inhuman.

(Wittgenstein, 1953)

Education is an admirable thing, but it is well to remember from time to time that nothing that is worth knowing can be taught.

(Oscar Wilde, 1891)

12.1 Introduction

It is important to remember that a completely risk-free IS project does not exist. IS risk management is about reducing risks, but it is never possible to entirely eliminate them.

IS risk management is not as complex as is sometimes thought. In fact, occasionally individuals are disappointed that there is not a greater collection of sophisticated tools and techniques available for the implementation of an IS risk management programme. It is sometimes thought that advanced mathematics or statistics need to be used to measure probabilities of all the events in order to understand and take control of IS project risks.

This is simply not true. Much of IS risk management is to do with the application of relatively straightforward and routine management procedures which help focus on potential problems. By giving these potential problems adequate attention they are either eliminated or the organisation goes some way to minimise the impact of these problems if they occur eventually. Perhaps the words of Tom Peters (1997) are relevant in this respect when he said:

Success in information management is 5% technology and 95% psychology.

For IS risk management to be successful it is essential to have several quite specific things in place. Some of these are to do with corporate culture and business attitudes while others are to do with business practices and processes. Of these two challenges, the corporate culture and business attitudes are the most difficult to work with and it is essential to get this right if appropriate changes are to be made.

The magnitude of the risk

Sometimes an IS development project fails because a risk develops into a large problem, while on other occasions the failure is due to a series of relatively small, or even trivial things, that all go wrong at the same time. In some respects this latter scenario is more dangerous to an IS development project than the former, as relatively small problems sometimes go unreported for a considerable length of time. In the case of the series of small problems the total of these small risks can in fact be much greater than their apparent sum.

12.2 Corporate culture and business attitudes

IS risk management requires the organisation to accept that the best laid plans will not necessarily be routinely achieved. It is important that the key players in the IS development project accept that actual performance can, and frequently does, differ quite materially from the original estimates. Of course, with the rather poor record of IS development projects not meeting deadlines or budgets, convincing the executives of this fact is not often difficult. However it can be quite challenging to obtain commitment to the expenditure of extra money and effort, to try to manage the reasons and causes, i.e. the risks that are responsible for these delays and budget over-runs. In reality, however IS risk management need not be expensive especially if it is integrated into the project management methodology. Furthermore when IS risk management is compared to the cost which it may avoid, it may easily be seen to earn a very attractive return.

12.3 Start discussing project success and failure

Where IS risk management has not yet been established as part of the organisation's project management methodology, it is important to have the organisation's development project record of success and failure put on the agenda for discussion. The simplest way of doing this is to create a log of all IS projects that have been initiated over the past two or three years and to establish how many of these have been on time and to budget. It will, of course, also be worth while noting, during this exercise, which of these IS projects have been abandoned before anything at all was delivered.

It is useful to start your IS risk management experience with a relatively small project and then progress to larger ones.

12.4 Emphasise the payback

IS risk management programmes are not especially costly but the potential to avoid waste and to deliver systems on time and within budget is very substantial. Thus there can be a very high return from a IS risk management programme and this needs to be emphasised and debated. Individuals who have been involved with problematic or failed projects may help motivate a risk management programme as they may be easily able to see how such a program would have helped their situation.

The Money Rule

Never spend more on reducing or eliminating a risk than the risk will cost if it materialises. There needs to be a strong focus on this rule if an IS project risk management program is to stay focused and save the organisation expense.

Of course some outlay will be required and this needs to be budgeted for in the project's costs. The level of expenditure on an IS risk management programme will vary enormously depending on the project, but in all cases it should not be a material amount of the project cost. For medium to large-sized projects about 1% of the budget could suffice as the cost of the IS risk management programme itself. However this amount of money has nothing to do with the amount which might be expended to avoid or eliminate a risk. It should be recalled that the cost of avoiding a or eliminating a risk should not exceed the expense which will be incurred if the risk actually materialises.

A stitch in time

IS project risks can quickly magnify if prompt action is not taken, therefore a effective IS project risk management programme implies a degree of empowerment. If delays are sustained in responding to a problematical situation then the knock-on or ripple effects have the opportunity to produce a greater impact on the project than if they are attended to immediately. Thus in IS project risk management a stitch in time may certainly save nine.

12.5 Know your IS department

As discussed in the early chapters of this book it is important to know the organisation and the capabilities of the IS department. Thus before embarking on a risk assessment, it is important to reflect on issues such as the maturity of the IS department as well as the possibility that there may be risks due to poor conceptualisation of the project. These are cornerstone issues and need considerable thought and attention. The less mature or the more uncertain is the senior management of the IS department, the more attention needs to be given to the issue of IS risk management. Where this immaturity is a big concern then outsourcing may be the only effective way of coping with the risk. In a similar way the organisation's own attitude to risk needs to be taken into account.

As discussed in Chapter 3 some organisations are risk averse while others are risk tolerant or even risk inclined. Any IS risk management programme needs to be cognisant of these attitudes and, as is the case in most organisations, where risk averseness is strong, appropriate management action should be taken.

12.6 Risk management and project management

As has been pointed out from the outset of this book, IS risk management needs to be seen as a part of Project Management and it needs to be integrated into the project management process. This was illustrated in Figure 1.1 where the risk issue was shown as requiring attention in the feasibility part of the SDLC. However it is not at the case that this is the only time when it is appropriate to initiate an IS risk management programme. At any stage in the project, especially if the stakeholders feel that the project is not quite going to plan, a IS risk management review should be performed.

It is also important that the IS risk management officer is an experienced and senior member of the project team. His or her voice needs to be heard above the general hustle and bustle of the day-to-day concerns of the project. If a junior person without experience and status is appointed to this job then it is much more difficult to make a success of it.

Some project management methodologies actually have risk management programmes or procedures built into them. If this is the case then it is just as well to start the organisation's experience of IS risk management by following such a programme. If this is not the case then the approach outlined in this book is sufficiently comprehensive to act as a model.

12.7 Research is central

The more that is known about the organisation, the IS department and the specific project, the more successful risk management will be. Identifying the stakeholders and understanding their requirements and attitudes will also help immensely.

Successful risk management implies that an open-door policy is in place so that any stakeholder can at any time raise concerns about the way the project is proceeding. This is not always popular as it can be seem by some IS development people as leading to scope creep.

The question of subsidiarity

It is important that actions that are taken to reduce a risk or to ameliorate the effect of a risk, should be taken at the appropriate level of management, or by the appropriate project officer. If IS project risk management is only handled by the project manager, appropriate decisions may not be made. Any appropriate stakeholder should be in a position to assist in reducing the project's risks when they become visible. This will produce the most effective IS project risk programme.

12.8 Regular reviews and audits

Finally, regular reviews and audits are essential, as all projects will at some time go off track even if only very temporarily. A risk review or audit will help bring the project back on track again. One of the most effective approaches to reviews and audits is to use the formative evaluation approach. Formative evaluation is an iterative evaluation and decision-making process that continually influences decisions about the IS development process and thus the resulting system (Fink 1993; Love 1991), guiding the project towards an effective and acceptable solution for the organisation. Kumar (1990) describes formative evaluation as a process that produces information that is then fed back during systems development to help improve the product under development.

This evaluation process, which is ideal for IS risk management, is designed to be management driven but supported by the eventual users of the IT-based system. This has the effect of ensuring that the technology investment both enhances business performance, as prescribed by management, and is also easily usable and acceptable to the eventual users of the system and meets operational requirements. (Boyton and Zmud 1987; Kumar 1990; Silk 1990; Niederman et al. 1991; Earl 1992; Premkumar and King 1994; Kettinger and Lee 1995, Remenyi et al 1997).

12.9 A final note

It is never too early or too late to employ an IS risk management programme. So start now. It is only by doing that real learning takes place.

Key learning points in this chapter

- ❑ When beginning an IS risk management project be careful of cultural issues. Get dialogue about the costs and benefits of the programme going as early as possible.

- ❑ Make sure your IS risk management programme is integrated into your project management methodologies.

- ❑ Do research on your project and your organisation.

- ❑ Hold regular reviews and audits.

Practical action guidelines

Start your IS risk management programme now!

Appendix A

IS project risk assessment questionnaires and forms

Business issues

Business issues	Date:		Project reference:		
RISK ISSUES		BR*	Acceptable risk level 1 = Low 4 = High	Assessment 1 = Low 4 = High	Gap‡
Business questions					
Is there appropriate business architecture in place and does the project make business sense?		1			
Is there a suitable degree of strategic alignment and does the project support the business strategy?		1			
Is the business problem properly understood, as the project will fail or at least be delayed if not?		1			
How vulnerable is the business? If the project fails, will the business do so as well?		1			
Is there appropriate support from the key stakeholders and is the buy-in in place?		2			
Are political and personal relationships poor, as project failure may be desirable for political reasons?		2			
Do most users see the project as advantageous and is there stakeholder support?		2			
Are users uncommitted to the changes, as the project will not deliver anything the users will use or need?		2			
Are most users located in a single geographical area, because delays can be caused by time spent communicating with users?		2			
What existing procedures will the project change, as new procedures in addition to a new system, may prove too much?		3			
Is other organisational change likely during the project and will users be able to cope with the level of change?		3			
Have mechanisms which cope with change such as formative evaluation been put in place?		3			

Notes: * BR = Business risk.

‡The gap is calculated by subtracting the risk assessment from the acceptable risk level

Development issues	Date:		Project reference:		
RISK ISSUES	**DR***	**Acceptable risk level 1 = Low 4 = High**	**Assessment 1 = Low 4 = High**	**Gap**	
Development questions					
How large is the project relative to previous ones in the organisation? If it is too big it may not be implementable.	1				
Can the project be delayed due to disputes over a poorly defined and agreed approach?	1				
Is the project dependent upon third parties whose delays can prevent delivery?	1				
Does the design need a large group, as this can lead to a project too complex to be implemented?	1				
Is a 'big bang' implementation unavoidable, as volumes of transactions and of change can be underestimated?	1				
Are the users unfamiliar with the technology, as user resistance may delay implementation?	1				
How much of the project may be outsourced, which can reduce the risk?	2				
Is the design of the project dependent on very few people, as key personnel can leave and the project fail?	2				
Are individual project roles poorly defined, which can lead to duplications, omissions and conflicts?	2				
Are staff unable to commit sufficient time to the project, as delays can occur pending time required from key staff?	2				
Are the required skills unavailable, as extra costs will be incurred acquiring the required skills?	2				
Are some staff indispensable to the project as non-availability of key staff will directly impact delivery?	2				
Are appropriate development tools available?	3				
Are development tools compatible with each other?	3				
Is the quality of the existing data poor, as substantial data clean up impacts on time scale and/or feasibility?	3				

Note: * DR = Development risk

Architecture issues

Architecture issues	Date:	Project reference:		
RISK ISSUES	**AR***	**Acceptable risk level** 1 = Low 4 = High	**Assessment** 1 = Low 4 = High	**Gap**
Architecture questions				
Is bespoke programming a major part of the project, as such systems do not always fulfil all business requirements and/or are bug-ridden?	1			
Is there adequate competencies in the chosen technology?	1			
Is there readily available a pool of competent professionals who may be employed?	1			
Is the project technologically complex, as overcoming technical complexities causes delays?	1			
Is the technology well supported locally, as long delays for support can cause the technology to fail irreparably?	2			
Are the proposed vendors sound and what happens if they go bust?	2			
Is there a disaster recovery plan in place?	2			
Is new or untried technology being used, as a fundamental part of the project, as new technology can prove impossible to use successfully in the time scale?	3			
Is unfamiliar software being used, as software bugs can delay or prevent implementation?	3			
At what stage in the product life cycle is the technology?	3			

Note: * AR = Architecture risk

Business risk audit	Date of audit:		Project reference:		
Business risk questions	**BR**	**Assessment 1 = Low 4 = High**	**Risk changes**	**Actions required**	**Individual responsible**
Is there appropriate business architecture in place and does the project make business sense?	1				
Is there a suitable degree of strategic alignment and does the project support the business strategy?	1				
Is the business problem properly understood as the project will fail or be delayed if not?	1				
How vulnerable is the business? If the project fails, will the business also?	1				
Is there appropriate support from the key stakeholders and is the buy-in in place?					
Are political and personal relationships poor, as project failure may be desirable for political reasons?	2				
Do most users see the project as advantageous and is there stakeholder support?	2				
Are users uncommitted to the changes, as the project will not deliver anything the users will use or need?	2				
Are most users located in one geographical area, because delays can be caused by time spent communicating with users?	2				
What existing procedures will the project change, as new procedures in addition to a new system, may prove too much?	3				
Is other organisational change likely during the project and will users be able to cope with the level of change?	3				
Have mechanisms which cope with change such as formative evaluation been put in place?	3				

Development risk audit		Date of audit:	Project reference		
Development risk questions	**DR**	**Assessment** **1=Low** **4=High**	**Risk** **changes**	**Actions** **required**	**Individual** **responsible**
How large is the project relative to the size to which the organisation is accustomed? If it is too big it may not be implementable.	1				
Can the project be delayed due to disputes over a poorly defined and agreed approach? Is the project dependent upon third parties whose delays can prevent delivery?	1 1				
Can the design only be achieved by a large group, as this can lead to a project that is too complex to be implemented?	1				
Is a 'big bang' implementation unavoidable, as volumes of transactions and levels of change can be underestimated?	1				
Are the users unfamiliar with the technology, as user resistance may delay implementation?	1				
How much of the project may be outsourced, which can reduce the risk?	2				
Is the design of the project dependent on very few people, as key personnel can leave and the project will fail?	2				
Are individual project roles poorly defined, which can lead to duplications, omissions and conflicts?	2				
Are staff unable to commit sufficient time to the project, as delays can occur pending time required from key staff?	2				
Are the required skills unavailable, as extra costs will be incurred acquiring those skills?	2				
Are some staff indispensable to the project, as non-availability of key staff will directly impact delivery?	2				
Are appropriate development tools available?	3				
Are tools compatible with each other?	3				
Is the quality of the existing data poor, as substantial data clean up impacts on time scale and/or feasibility?	3				

Architecture risk audit	Date of audit:		Project Reference		
Architecture risk questions	AR	Assessment 1=Low 4=High	Risk changes	Actions required	Individual responsible
Is bespoke programming a major part of the project ,as such systems do not always fulfil all business requirements and/or are bug-ridden?	1				
Is there adequate competencies in the chosen technology?	1				
Is there readily available a pool of competent professionals who may be employed?	1				
Is the project technologically complex, as overcoming complexities causes delays?	1				
Is the technology well supported locally, as long delays for support can cause the technology to fail irreparably?	2				
Are the proposed vendors sound and what happens if they go bust?	2				
Is there a disaster recovery plan in place?	2				
Is new or untried technology being used as a fundamental part of the project, as new technology can prove impossible to use successfully in the time scale?	3				
Is unfamiliar software being used, as software bugs can delay or prevent implementation?	3				
At what stage in the product life cycle Is the technology?	3				

Business risk action plan	Date of audit:		Project reference		
Business risk questions	Actions required	Resources required	Date for action	Individual responsible	Outcome of action
Is there appropriate business architecture in place and does the project make business sense?					
Is there a suitable degree of strategic alignment and does the project support the business strategy?					
Is the business problem properly understood, as the project will fail or at least be delayed if not?					
How vulnerable is the business? If the project fails, will the business also?					
Is there appropriate support from the key stakeholders and is the buy-in in place?					
Are political and personal relationships poor, as project failure may be desirable for political reasons?					
Do most users see the project as advantageous and is there stakeholder support?					
Are users uncommitted to the changes, as the project delivers nothing for them?					
Are most users located in a single area, because delays can be caused by time spent communicating with users?					
What existing procedures will the project change, as new procedures in addition to a new system, may prove too much?					
Is other organisational change likely during the project and will users be able to cope with the level of change?					
Are mechanisms to cope with change such as formative evaluation in place?					

Development risk action plan	Date of audit:		Project reference		
Development risk questions	Actions required	Resources required	Date for action	Individual responsible	Outcome of action
How large is the project relative to the size to which the organisation is accustomed? If it is too big it may not be implementable.					
Can the project be delayed due to disputes over a poorly defined and agreed approach?					
Is the project dependent upon third parties whose delays can prevent delivery?					
Can the design only be achieved by a large group, as this can lead to a project that is too complex to be implemented?					
Is a 'big bang' implementation unavoidable, as volumes of transactions and levels of change can be underestimated?					
Are users unfamiliar with the technology, as user resistance may delay implementation?					
How much of the project may be outsourced, which can reduce the risk?					
Is the design dependent on very few people, as key personnel can leave and the project fail?					
Are individual project roles poorly defined, which can lead to duplications, omissions and conflicts?					
Are staff unable to commit sufficient time, as delays can occur pending time from key staff?					
Are the required skills unavailable, as extra costs will be incurred acquiring those skills?					
Are some staff indispensable, as non-availability of key staff will directly impact delivery?					
Are appropriate development tools available?					
Are the tools compatible with each other?					
Is the quality of the existing data poor, as substantial data clean up impacts time scale and/or feasibility?					

Architecture risk action plan	Date of audit:		Project reference		
Architecture risk questions	Actions required	Resources required	Date for action	Individual responsible	Outcome of action
Is bespoke programming a major part of the project, as such systems do not always fulfil all business requirements and/or are bug-ridden?					
Is there adequate competencies in the chosen technology?					
Is there readily available a pool of competent professionals who may be employed?					
Is the project technologically complex, as overcoming technical complexities causes delays?					
Is the technology well supported locally, as long delays for support can cause the technology to fail irreparably?					
Are the proposed vendors sound and what happens if they go bust?					
Is there a disaster recovery plan in place?					
Is new or untried technology being used as a fundamental part of the project, as new technology can prove impossible to use successfully in the time scale?					
Is unfamiliar software being used, as software bugs can delay or prevent implementation?					
At what stage in the product life cycle is the technology?					

Graphical representation of risk assessment

Date:	Project Reference:	Review No.

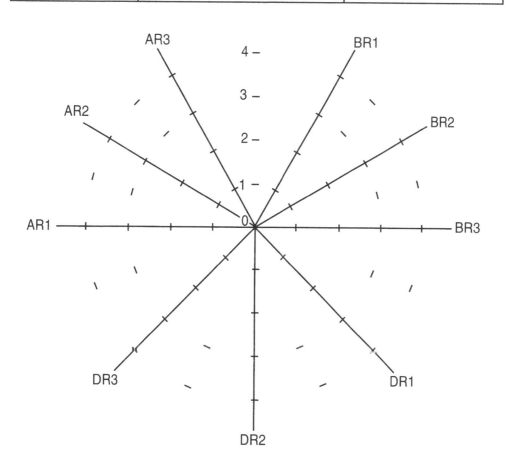

Blank jigsaw

Date:	Project reference:	Review no.

The seriousness/probability of the damage assessment rating form

Consequence issues seriousness	Date:		Project Reference:							
Rate the *seriousness* of each consequence where 1 is not serious and 10 is very serious										
	1	2	3	4	5	6	7	8	9	10
Mismatch and waste (*mw*)										
IS islands (*ii*)										
Loss of fit or relevance (*lf*)										
Aggro and distrust (*ad*)										
Learning curve & delays (*lc*)										
Rework (*rw*)										
Quality reduction (*qr*)										
Instability (*is*)										
Dilution of business advantages (*db*)										

Appendix B

Glossary of terms

Benefit

A term used to indicate an advantage, profit or gain attained by an individual or organisation.

Business vision

The business vision is what the management want to achieve with the enterprise in the future. A business vision usually refers to the medium to long term. It is often expressed in terms of a series of objectives.

Capital investment

Funds committed to long-term assets within the firm such as land and building, plant and equipment or computer hardware. In some cases computer software is even regarded as a capital investment.

Competitive advantage

This term is usually used to describe how one particular organisation attracts clients or customers when in competition with another. There are various sources of competitive advantage including low cost and differentiation.

Cost benefit analysis

The process of comparing the various costs associated with an investment with the benefits and the profits which it generates. Cost benefit analysis attempts to demonstrate whether the investment will earn a sufficient return in order for the organisation to consider it to be economically worth while. There are a number of different approaches to cost benefit analysis including, cost displacement, cost avoidance, risk analysis, etc.

CSF (Critical Success Factors)

Those aspects of the business that must be right for the enterprise to succeed in achieving its objectives. It is also sometimes said that even though all other aspects of the business are going well, if the critical success factors are not, then the business will not succeed.

Formative evaluation

Formative evaluation is an iterative evaluation and decision making process continually influencing decisions about the information systems development process and the resulting information system The term 'formative evaluation' has its origins in the evaluation of educational programmes and social programmes (Scriven 1967; Stake 1975, 1983; Patton 1986).

The phenomenon of formative evaluation is not new (Chelimsky 1985). It has been applied for many years in a number of disciplines with the roots of the concept stretching back into the nineteenth century. The meaning of the word, taken from the Oxford Dictionary, is to 'mould by discipline and education'. This is very close to the approach used by Walsham (1993) which he refers to as interpretative evaluation and which he highlights as an important facet in information systems management.

Hard cost

Costs associated with an investment that are agreed by everyone to be directly attributable to the investment, and which can be easily captured by accounting procedures.

Hidden cost

A non-obvious cost associated with an investment that may in fact appear to be due to another source.

IT business benefits

This normally refers to advantages, profits or gains delivered by the use of information systems. This traditionally involves performing tasks faster, with fewer errors and producing higher quality output than could otherwise be achieved.

Intangible benefit

Benefits produced by investments that are not immediately obvious and/or measurable.

IT benefit

The benefit produced by an investment in information technology. It is likely that such an investment will produce both tangible and intangible IT benefits.

Opportunity cost

The opportunity cost of an investment is the amount the organisation could have earned if the sum invested in IT was used in another way.

Payback

The amount of time, usually expressed in years and months, required for an original investment to be repaid by the cash-in flows.

ROI (Return on Investment)

Accounting or financial management term to describe how well the firm has used its resources. It is usually calculated by dividing net profit after tax by total net assets.

Risk analysis

A technique used to assess the potential profitability of an investment. It involves the use of ranges as input variables rather than single-point estimates. Probabilities may be associated with these ranges. The output of risk analysis is a profile of a series of possible results.

Soft cost

Costs associated with an investment that are not readily agreed by everyone to be directly attributable to the investment, and which are not easily captured by accounting procedures.

Strategic vision

How the top management of an enterprise believes it can achieve its objectives in the medium to long-term.

Strategy

The formal use of this word refers to the way a firm finds, gets and keeps its clients. Common usage has reduced the meaning of strategy to be synonymous with plan.

Summative evaluation

According to Finne et al (1995) summative evaluation approaches typically aim at assessing outcomes and impacts; they take place towards the end of the programme or after its conclusion. They go on to point out that summative evaluations may be used conceptually, instrumentally, or persuasively. This means that the results of such an evaluation may be used to reconsider an investment proposal, to redirect investment efforts or to convince others that a new course of action is required.

Tangible benefit

Benefits produced by an investment that are immediately obvious and measurable.

Vision

Sometimes referred to as Strategic Vision or Business Vision, this term refers to a view as to how the firm can successfully function in the marketplace in the medium- to long-term. It usually encompasses how the firm will find, get and keep its clients.

Appendix C

Financial measures used in cost benefit analysis

Payback

The payback may be defined as the amount of time, usually expressed in years and months, required for the original investment amount to be repaid by the cash-in flows. This measure is sometimes used with nominal cash-in flows and sometimes used with discounted cash-in flows. Nominal cash flows are the amounts unadjusted for the time value of money. The most popular form of payback used today is referred to as the exhaust method. The exhaust method of payback calculation involves the deduction of each year's cash-in flow from the original investment until the original amount is reduced to zero. This method should be contrasted with the average payback method which only gives a rough approximation of the period of time required to recover the investment amount when the cash-in flows are relatively constant.

Exhaust method

Payback in time (years,months,etc) = Investment – Cumulative benefit

The calculation of the payback by the exhaust method is a reiterative process which requires the cumulative benefit to be subtracted from the investment until the result is zero. The time at which the result is zero represents the period which is required for the investment amount to be returned.

Average method

$$\text{Payback in time} \ = \ \frac{\text{Investment}}{\text{Average annual benefit}}$$

This average method is only useful if the annual benefits do not materially vary from the average. If there is any substantial variability in the annual benefits this method will produce meaningless results. Many firms use the payback as the primary criterion for deciding whether an investment is suitable or not.

It is generally considered that the cash flows used to calculate the payback should have first been discounted. This is referred to as a discounted payback. If this is done it will produce a time-value-based payback measure which will reflect the cost of capital. A discounted payback will always show a longer period than one based on nominal values.

Net present value (NPV)

The net present value may be defined as the difference between the sum of the values of the cash-in flows, discounted at an appropriate cost of capital, and the present value of the original investment. Provided the NPV is greater than or equal to zero the investment will earn the firm's required rate of return. The size of the NPV may be considered as either a measure of the surplus which the investment makes over its required return, or as a margin of error in the size of the investment amount.

$$\text{Present value of benefit} \ = \ \frac{\text{Benefit}}{(1+i)^n}$$

Where i = rate of interest
          n = number of years

NPV = Σ Present value of benefit − Present value of investment

The interpretation of the NPV should be based on the rules:

If NPV >= 0 then invest
If NPV < 0 then do not invest

The size of the NPV represents the margin of error which may be made in the estimate of the investment amount before the investment will be rejected.

Profitability index (PI)

The profitability index is defined as the sum of the present values of the cash-in flows divided by the present value of the investment. This shows a rate of return expressed as the number of discounted pounds and pence which the investment will earn for every pound originally invested.

$$PI = \frac{\Sigma \text{ Present value of benefits}}{\text{Present value of investment}}$$

Internal rate of return (IRR)

The internal rate of return is the rate of interest which will cause the NPV to be zero. It is the internally generated return which the investment will earn throughout its life. It is also frequently referred to as the yield of the investment.

$$IRR = i \text{ such that } NPV = 0$$

Rate of return or return on investment (ROI)

The rate of return or return on investment, which is sometimes referred to as the simple return on investment, is calculated by considering the annual benefit divided by the investment amount. Sometimes an average rate of return for the whole period of investment is calculated by averaging the annual benefits while on other occasions the rate of return is calculated on a year by year basis using individual benefit amounts.

$$ROI = \frac{\text{Annual benefit}}{\text{Investment amount}}$$

Appendix D

List of acronyms

AA	Architectural action
AC	Architectural consequence
AR	Architectural risk
BA	Business action
BC	Business consequence
BR	Business risk
CASE	Computer aided systems engineering
CBA	Cost benefit analysis
CIO	Chief information officer
CSF	Critical success factors
DA	Development action
DC	Development consequence
DCF	Discounted cash flow
DR	Development risk
IRR	Internal rate of return
IS	Information system
ISD	Information systems department
IT	Information technology
ITB	Information technology budget

ITA   Information technology architecture

NPV   Net present value

PI   Profitability index

PIA   Post implementation audit

R&D   Research and development

RAD   Rapid application development

ROI   Return on investment

SD   Standard deviation

SDLC   Software development life cycle

SIS   Strategic information system

SISP   Strategic information system plan

Appendix E

IT architecture

An overall IT architecture is needed to assist in the delivery of effective information systems because such information systems require corporate-wide policies and guidelines which optimise information systems capabilities and minimise misunderstandings, redundancy and information systems inconsistency.

An information technology architecture (ITA) plan has as its primary objective the establishment of the firm's long-term technology infrastructure which will allow systems to be designed and implemented in an effective and efficient way. ITA seeks to avoid fragmentation, redundancy and inconsistency. It defines components, formats, structure, and interfaces. The importance with which the ITA is regarded is often seen as a measure of the firm's IT status, direction and strategy.

An ITA shows where the firm is headed and what structures need to be in place before it can achieve its long term objectives. Without such a plan, as computerisation proceeds, the technical environment may become diverse, uncontrolled and inefficient. An ITA puts into place policies and standards so that hardware functions effectively and software allows access for system management and control. ITA planning is one of the most important roles of the chief information officer (CIO). An ITA requires input from other information systems stakeholders as well. It is far too important to be left to the technologists alone.

It is not easy to precisely define the term information technology architecture. An ITA has been described as the structure of IT within the enterprise, which has been developed with the specific purpose of facilitating the firm's business objectives. It refers to all the different aspects of IT within the enterprise and not just the centralised information systems. The meaning of an ITA may be better understood by looking at the Shorter Oxford English Dictionary definition of architecture which states *inter alia* that architecture is the art and science of developing plans (for any building, structure or system). Thus the ITA is the art and science of developing plans for the deployment of information technology in its broadest sense. By their nature these plans and policies will extend beyond the short term to the medium and even long term.

An important aspect of an ITA is that it deals with the structure in which the different aspects of the firm's information technology exist. Its aim is to enable the enterprise to carry out its business in new ways which have strategic potential far beyond the traditional role of simple administrative systems. An ITA differs from other forms of information systems planning such as an IT budget or even a Strategic Information Systems Plan (SISP) in that it takes a much longer view of the IT function in the firm, usually looking ahead between three and five and in some cases, even ten years. Also an ITA focuses on the standards which the firm needs to have in place to allow IS to develop efficiently and effectively. Thus correctly developed and communicated, an ITA may play an important role in reducing the development risks associated with an information systems project.

Appendix F

References and bibliography

Accola, W. L. (1994) 'Assessing Risk and Uncertainty in New Technology Investments', *Accounting Horizons*, vol. 8, no. 3, September.

Allingham, P. and O'Connor, M. (1992) 'MIS Success: Why does it vary among users?', *Journal of Information Technology*, vol. 1. pp. 160-168.

Bashein, B. J. Markus, M. L. and Riley, P. (1994) 'Preconditions for BPR Success And How to Prevent Failures', *Information Systems Management*, Spring, pp. 7-13.

Beam., K. (ed) (1994) 'Software Engineering Productivity and Quality', in IS Analyser, vol. 32, no. 2.

Bernstein, P. (1996) *Against the Gods*, Wiley and Sons, New York.

Berny, J. and Townsend, P. (1993) 'Macrosimulation of Project Risks a Practical Way Forward', *International Journal of Project Management*, vol. 11, no. 4, November.

Betts, M. (1992) 'Feds Debate Handling of Failing IT Projects', Computerworld, 2 November.

Boyadjian and Warren (1987) *Risks, Reading Corporate Signals*, Wiley and Sons, Chichester.

Boyton, A.C. and Zmud, R.W. (1987) 'Information Technology Planning in the 1990s: Directions for Practice and Research', MIS Quarterly, March, pp. 59-71.

Butler Cox (1990) Proceedings of the Butler Cox Management Conference: Value from Information Technology: The Business Perspectives; Plenary Session; Day 1; Butler Cox London.

Cash, J. I., McFarlan, F. W. and McKenney, J. L. (1992) *Corporate Information Systems Management: The Issues Facing Senior Executives*, third edition, Irwin, Boston, Massachusetts.

Chapman, C. and Ward, S. (1997) *Project Risk Management*, Wiley and Sons, Chichester.

Chesterton, G.K. (1968) *The Napoleon of Notting Hill*, Bodley Head, London (first published 1904).

Collins H. (1994) A broadcast video on Science Matters entitled *Does Science Matter*, Open University, BBC, United Kingdom.

Collins, H. and Pinch, T. (1994) *The Golem*, Cambridge University Press, New York.

Correia, C. et al. (1989) *Financial Management*, second edition, Juta & Co., Cape Town.

Crescenzi, A.D. (1988) 'The Dark Side of Strategic IS Implementation', *Information Strategy: The Executives Journal*, 1988, Fall, pp 14 – 20.

Crockford, N. (1980) *An Introduction to Risk Management*, Woodhead-Faulkner Ltd, Cambridge, UK.

Davenport, T. (1993) *Process Innovation: Reengineering Work through Information Technology*, Harvard Business School Press, Cambridge, MA.

Davidow, W.H. and Malone, M.S. (1992) *The Virtual Corporation*, Harper Collins, New York.

De Marco, T. (1982) *Controlling Software Projects*, Yourdon Press, New York.

Dickson, G. (1989) 'Risk Management : What Does The Future Hold?', *Journal of the Society of Fellows, London*, Chartered Insurance Institute, vol. 4, July.

Doherty, N.A. (1985) *Corporate Risk Management – A Financial Exposition*, McGraw-Hill Inc., New York.

Drucker, P. F. (1955), cited in Kennedy, C. (1994) *The Practice of Management*, Heinemann, London, Harper & Row , New York.

Earl, M. J. (1992) 'Putting IT in its Place: a Polemic for the Nineties', *Journal of Information Technology*, vol. 7.

Einstein, Albert (1934) *The World as I See It*, Covici Friede, New York.

Emery, J. (1991) 'Reengineering the Organisation', *MIS Quarterly*, March.

Fairley R. (1990) 'Risk Management: The Key to Successful Software Projects', in *Experiences with the management of software projects*, Workshop Series, no 9.

Fayol, H. (1949) cited in Valsamakis et al. (1992) *General and industrial management*, Pitman Publishing Corporation, New York. (English translation of the French original published in 1916).

Felice, Frank A. (1987) *The Principles of Economics*, cited in *RISKS, Reading Corporate Signals*, Boyadjian and Warren, 1987, Wiley and Sons, Chichester.

Fink, A. (1993) *Evaluation Fundamentals – Guiding Health Programs, Research and Policy*, Sage Publications, Newbury Park CA.

Foster, R. (1986) *Innovation – the Attackers' Advantage*, Summit Books, New York.

Gladden, G.R. (1982) 'Stop the Life-Cycle, I want to get off', *ACM SIGSOFT Software Engineering notes*, vol. 7, no. 2, pp. 35 – 39.

Gonin, S. J. and Money, A. H. (1989) *Nonlinear L_p Norm Estimation*, Marcel Dekker.

Green, J. (1989) *The Macmillan Dictionary of Contemporary Quotations*, Macmillan, London.

Greene, M.R. and Serbein, O. N. (1983) *Risk management : Text and Cases*, Reson Publishing Co., Reston, Virginia.

Grindley, K. (1991) *Managing IT At Board Level*, Pitman Publishing, London.

Hammer, M. and Champy, J. (1993) *Reengineering the Corporation : A Manifesto for Business Revolution*, Nicholas Brealey Publishing, London.

Handy, C. (1989) *The Age of Unreason*, Arrow Books, p. 71.

Harvey-Jones, J. (1988) *Making it Happen – Reflections on Leadership*, Fontana Collins, London.

Haspeslaugh, P. (1982) cited in Accola, W. L. (1994), 'Portfolio Planning: Uses and Limits', *Harvard Business Review* 60, Jan-Feb, pp. 58–74.

Howard, L.S. (1994) 'Business process reengineering; Impacts; Risk management; Risk assessment', *National Underwriter*, vol. 98, iss. 41, October 10.

Johnson, N.L. and Kotz, S. (1970) *Distributions in Statistics: Continuous Distributions, vols 1 and 2*, Houghton Mifflin.

Kanter, R.M. (1989) cited in Kennedy, C. (1994), *When Giants Learn to Dance*, Simon & Schuster, New York.

Keil, M. (1994) 'Managing IT projects for success: Re-engineering or Better project management?', ICIS panel discussion, Vancouver, 16 December.

Kennedy, C. (1994) *Managing with the GURUS*. Century Business Books, Random House, Johannesburg.

Kettinger, W.J. and Lee, C.C. (1995) 'Perceived Service Quality and User Satisfaction with the Information Services Function', Decision Sciences, vol. 25, no. 5/6, pp. 737–765.

Keynes, J.M. (1964) *The General Theory of Employment, Interest and Money*, Harcourt Brace, Jovanovich, San Diego (first published 1936).

Kumar, K. (1990) 'Post Implementation Evaluation of Computer Based Information Systems: Current Practices', Communications of the ACM, vol. 33, no 2, pp. 203–212, February.

Laudon, K.A. (1989) *A General Model for Understanding the Relationship between Information Technology and Organizations*, New York University, Center for Research on Information Systems, New York.

Lightle, S. and Sprohge, H. (1992) 'Strategic Information System Risk', *Internal Auditing*, Summer.

Logue, D. E. (1981) cited in Accola, W. L. (1994) 'Some Thoughts on Corporate Investment Strategy and Pure Strategic Investments'. *Readings in Strategy for Corporate Investment*, edited by F. G. J. Derkinderen and R. L. Crum, Pitman, Boston, MA.

Love, A. (1991) 'Internal Evaluation: Building Organisations from Within', Applied Social Research Methods Series, vol. 24, Sage Publications, Newbury Park CA.

Lyytinen, K. (1988) 'Expectation Failure Concept and Systems Analysts' View of Information Systems Failures: Results of an Exploratory Study', *Information & Management*, vol. 14, pp. 45–46.

Lyytinen, K. and Hirscheim, R. (1987) 'Information Systems Failures – a Study and Classificiation of the Empirical Literature', in P.I. Zorkoczy, (ed.) Oxford Surveys in Information Technology, vol. 4, Oxford University Press, Oxford, pp. 257–309.

McFarlan, F.W. cited by Ewusi-Mensah, K. and Przasnyski, Z.H. (1991) 'On Information Systems Project Abandonment: An Exploratory Study of Organisational Practices', *MIS Quarterly*, March, pp.67-83.

McFarlan, F.W. (1990) A video produced on the subject of information management, Harvard Business School.

McFarlan, F.W. (1994) Unplublished paper presented at the University of the Witwatersrand, Johannesburg.

McGaughey, R.E.Jr., Snyder, C.A. and Carr, H.H. (1994) 'Implementing Information Technology for Competitive Advantage : Risk Management Issues'. *Information and Management.* vol. 26. pp. 273–280.

Medawar, P. (1986) *The Limits of Science*, Oxford University Press, Oxford.

Neider, Charles (ed.) (1953) *Mark Twain Autobiography*, quoted in *The Columbia Dictionary of Quotations*, Columbia University Press,1995.

Neiderman, F., Brancheau, J.C. and Wetherbe, J.C. (1991) 'Information Systems Management Issues for the 1990s', MIS Quarterly, vol. 15, no. 4, pp. 475–500.

Nugus, S. (1997) Financial Planning with Spreadsheets – Forecasting, Planning and Budgeting, Kogan Page, London.

Peters, T. (1987) *Thriving on Chaos*, McMillan Publishers.

Poppel, H.L. and Goldstein, B. (1987) *Information Technology: The Trillion-Dollar Opportunity*, McGraw-Hill.

Porter, M. (1985) Competitive Advantage, The Free Press, New York.

Premkumar, G. and King, W.R. (1994) 'Organisational Characteristics and Information Systems Planning: an Empirical Study', Information Systems Research, vol. 5, no. 2, June, pp. 75–109.

Remenyi, D.S.J. (1993) *Information Management Case Studies*, Pitman Publishing, London.

Remenyi, D.S.J. (1991) *Introducing Strategic Information Systems Planning*, NCC Blackwell, Oxford.

Remenyi, D.S.J., Money, A. and Twite, A. (1995 & 1998) *The effective measurement and management of IT costs and benefits*, Butterworth Heinemann, Oxford.

Remenyi, D.S.J. and Sherwood-Smith, M. (1998:c) 'An active benefits realisation approach to information systems project management', working paper, Department of Information Systems, University of the Witwatersrand, Johannesburg.

Romney, M. (1994) 'Business Process Re-engineering'. *The CPA Journal*, October, pp. 30–33.

Schneider, B., Gunnarson, S.K. and Niles-Jolly, K. (1994) 'Creating the Climate and Culture of Success', *Organizational Dynamics*, Summer, pp. 17–28.

Senge, P. (1992) *The Fifth Discipline*, Random House, Sydney.

Silk, D.J. (1990) 'Managing IS Benefits for the 1990s', Journal of Information Technology, vol. 5.

Short, J.E. and Venkatraman, N. (1992) cited in Remenyi (1993). 'Beyond Business Process Redesign: Redefining Baxter's Business Network', *Sloan Management Review*, Fall.

Tampoe, M. (1993) 'Motivating Knowledge Workers: The Challenge of the 1990s'. *Long Range Planning*, vol. 26, no. 3 pp. 49–55

Turner, J.R. (1993) *The Handbook of Project-Based Management*, McGraw Hill, Maidenhead.

Umbaugh, R. (1992) "On the Strategic Value of Information Systems", *Information Systems Management*, Summer.

Valsamakis, A.C., Vivian, R.W. and du Toit, G.S. (1992) *The theory and principles of risk management.* Butterworth Publishers, Durban.

Wiersema, F. (1996) *Customer Intimacy*, Knowledge Exchange, Santa Monica, CA.

Willocks, L. and Griffiths, C. (1994) *Beyond 2000: The Source Book for Major Projects*, The Major Projects Society, Templeton College, Oxford.

Wittgenstein, L. (1980), *Culture and Value*, ed. by G. H. von Wright with Heikki Nyman.

Zadjlic, W. (1986) cited in Valsamakis et al (1992) *The Future of Risk Management* Risk Research Group. London.

Peters, Tom, Forbes, A.S.A.P. cited by Davenport T (1997) in *Information Ecology – Mastering the Information and Knowledge Environment*, Oxford University Press, New York.

Index

Printed and bound by CPI Group (UK) Ltd, Croydon, CR0 4YY

17/10/2024

01775697-0003